THE MAKING OF MAN

THE MAKING OF MAN

Essays in the Christian Spirit

by
Christopher F. Mooney, S.J.

15737

PAULIST PRESS
New York / Paramus / Toronto

*To the Faculty and Students of
Woodstock College*

Contents

Introduction

"Divine revelation," writes Bernard Lonergan, "is God's entry into man's making of man." [1] This succinct statement well summarizes the thinking taking place today in the Christian churches. The whole of modern culture is concerned with the making of man, and what the churches have realized is that the Christian message is essentially a proclamation that God has entered into this making, supporting it, directing it, healing it. Hence the contemporary theological emphasis upon the larger implications of the momentous fact of the Incarnation. Christianity proclaims that in Christ the human ideal for which all men strive has actually been realized in history; that unless one is a man as Christ was a man, one cannot be a man at all. Christ was indeed a whole man, an integral man, all that men have ever hoped to be. He had a body like ours, a mind, free will, sensitivity, all our nature's wonderful capacity for love and joy and thought and suffering. Yet though human nature remained in him all that it was, it ceased to be a complete whole, it lost that independence proper to a creature with an intrinsic finality of its own. For Christ was perfect man precisely because he was perfect God. So total and intimate is the union between Christ's human nature and the Word of God, that never for all eternity will that human nature belong to itself.

The Incarnation thus posits the problem of human life in new terms. As John Courtney Murray well said, the problem is now not how to be a man, but how to be more than a man. In his own person Christ showed that a man can be himself only when he is one with God, and to dream any longer of being merely a man is to refuse to be totally human. "Man's aspirations after self-completion must carry him to acceptance of the divinizing grace of Christ, or they are doomed to sterility. Historically man's nature has been opened to a share in divinity; it cannot close itself, and it attempts

1

to do so on peril of self-destruction. . . . To become human we must consent to be made divine." [2] The true Christian must freely acknowledge, then, as St. Paul insists so strongly, that all his moral worth is a pure gift, enabling him to reach a human fulfillment otherwise out of his reach. And the greater perfection he achieves as a man, the more he has received from God. Nor does God's eagerness to give make all this any less gratuitous. "We are his design; God has created us in Christ Jesus, pledged to such good actions as he has prepared beforehand to be the employment of our lives." [3] The joy of the Christian is founded precisely on this divine initiative which transports him into a sphere that is God's alone, giving him in and through Christ a share in divine life.

Clearly this fundamental truth of Christian faith can have momentous psychological consequences. Man's natural desire for self-sufficiency, the making of himself by himself, must now be abdicated, and he must recognize once and for all that his integration as a person is not solely the achievement of his own desires but is initially a work of God. This is no easy matter. Natural life in us prefers to keep well away from anything better or stronger or higher than itself, anything that might make it feel small—like the obstinate tin soldiers of C. S. Lewis, who wanted to be left to themselves and have nothing to do with flesh and blood, because all they could see was their tin being spoiled. Significantly enough it is to this fundamental impulse that Thomas Aquinas attributes the origin and essence of all sin, namely the desire not so much to be equal to God as to be under no obligation to him, to escape from his bounty, to rely on one's own powers and to seek one's happiness by oneself.[4] The Christian, on the other hand, must acknowledge that Christ is truly at the very center of his life, and that he must love Christ enough to want to be united to him. Otherwise, how could anyone tolerate the thought of being bound to another, not only in living and acting, but in the very substance of one's being? It is thus no small achievement to grasp with one's whole intellectual and moral dynamism the beauty of that overwhelming truth, that to seek one's true self apart from the love of Christ is to search in vain for a peace that cannot be found and for a fulfillment which does not exist.

The Incarnation, however, tells us not only what man is

destined to be, but also what he must strive to do. For Christ entered into human history and remained within it for thirty years, subject to the same human, physical and cosmic forces which we grapple with today. To live and work in time, therefore, to explore the human and the material, is to do what he did and to explore what he explored. Hence the divine plan for man cannot be considered independently of God's design for the natural in his creation. God wills not only man's divinization, but likewise his perfection here on earth as man, the growth of his intellect, his dominion over the material world and even other planets through science and technology, the development of all his social institutions, domestic, national, international. These enterprises man must accomplish on his own initiative, transforming with his God-given talents the world which his Father has made for him. This is not to say that these human ideals are themselves salvific, or that they directly contribute to the kingdom of God. This God alone can achieve, though it should be noted that his unmerited intervention always takes place in and through the events of human history. Nor is it to imply that such ideals can ever escape frustration and even subversion from the sinfulness of man. It is simply to assert that they are human, and as such objects of a divine will. These are the ends and values proper to earth and time, neither final nor supreme, but autonomous in their own sphere, and well worthy of the energies of Christian man as long as he is a citizen of this world.

In and through the Incarnation, therefore, the Christian gains a perspective which affirms, supports, and enlarges all his genuinely human desires. It is this synthesis of values in the Christian's faith, its value for eternal life and its value for temporal life, which is one of the cardinal contemporary lessons that man must learn. "What the Church ultimately wants in the temporal order," wrote John Courtney Murray, "is to see there reflected, in civic friendship, the spirit of charity that is the primary expression of her faith. She wants this for the sake of the city, as essential to its good; she wants it too as the necessary expression of her own faith. . . . Love of the city's common good, with the faith in goodness that it implies, is itself an inchoative form of the love of the true God who is goodness itself." [5] Abstractly considered, there seem to be no two ways of life more opposed than the humanistic way of making all things tributary to man and the religious way of making man entirely tributary to God. But as Newman saw so clearly, they are only opposed as the left leg is to the right. Taken together they enable the Christian to cease halting and to walk, to fulfill his own nature and to place that nature fully developed at the service of God.[6]

From what has been said thus far, it will be clear that from a Christian perspective the making of man involves a double orientation, toward self-transcendence and toward human self-involvement. Historically this double orientation has been realized in the concrete body-person of Jesus, and it is for this reason that Karl Rahner has suggested that Christology can in large measure be regarded as a transcendent anthropology. For if the essence of man is to be unbounded, then the man who is man in the fullest sense *is* God's existence in the world.[7] Nor can it be claimed that such procedure will simply reduce Christology to anthropology. The witness of Christianity has always been that God's love for man and plan in Christ is universal, valid for all men everywhere throughout time, and not open to option or revision by man himself. To begin with man, therefore, is legitimate theologically, since we then study precisely what Christianity is bearing witness to. Man's self-understanding thus becomes as intrinsic to theology as the data of revelation itself. This is why Edward Schillebeeckx can write that it is "impossible to formulate any statement about God which does not at the same time say something meaningful about man himself, or any statement about man which does not say something meaningful about God." [8] All that God has wanted to say he has said in Jesus. But this is surely more than the *kerygma.* A man saved from drowning, to use Barth's image, does indeed reflect upon and speak about his rescue, but his task in life is nonetheless to love and work and achieve as a rescued man. As a consequence human culture becomes necessarily related to the *kerygma,* and the object of theology becomes precisely this relationship.

Now one of the major tasks of theology today is to show how the Christian experience takes place in and through the human experience. To be a Christian means not to be molded into some ecclesiastical form, but to be freed to become one's authentic human self. In this sense there are no religious experiences, only human experiences interpreted from a Christian point of view. This point of view, however, makes all the difference in the world. For not every experience of man is necessarily a human experience nor every material achievement a genuinely human one. The manipulation of human emotions and desires by entertainment media and advertising, for example, may in fact degrade man by appealing to his psychological weakness and even disrupting his personality. In the same way, the knowledge gained by science and its practical use through technology can be used not to expand man's primacy in the world but to subordinate him to a machine. Everything depends, therefore, upon whether values proper to man are given the primacy. If they are, then the experience and achievement in question become in the deepest sense Christian, for they contain, at least implicitly, a reference to the transcendent. Man, says Michael Ramsey, "will meet the numinous and reverence it not only in the consciously religious God-man relationship but within the ups and downs of human life. It is within human life, and indeed within the non-religious aspects of human life, that many of the phenomena which we call transcendence occur. Transcendence is seen in human actions which are terrifying—perhaps terrifying in generosity, in forgiveness, in self giving, in acts of selfless identification with human misery. Here is seen *mysterium tremendum et fascinans,* a beyondness which tells of another world." [9]

Such acknowledgment of mystery in man beyond a mere naturalistic image is indeed a prelude to conversion, to *metanoia.* It is capable of setting in motion a whole series of interlocked changes by which a man comes to share not only in the fullness of Christ's humanity, but also in the fullness of his redemption. Through contact with the passion, death and resurrection of Christ man is liberated and given power not only to overcome the dominion of sin in his life but also to transmute into virtue the mordant effects of sin, suffering and death. Such a man can then find in human anguish a sign of annunciation, for he yields himself to him who assuaged all anguish by turning it into hope.

"In all this we are conquerers, through him who granted us his love." [10] There is a bias in man, said Chesterton, like the bias of a bowl: when he goes straight, he goes crooked. No true humanism can be built except upon a recognition of one's own capacity to be a traitor, both to God and to one's fellow men. The mysteries of Incarnation and redemption must thus be preserved as a psychological as well as an objective unity if the Christian is to be capable at one and the same time of avoiding defeatism and discouraging the optimism of unrealistic utopias. In Christ alone does he find him "whom God gave us to be all our wisdom, our justification, our sanctification, and our atonement." [11]

The nine essays which follow attempt to further theology's contemporary task of showing how Christian and human coincide. They accordingly seek to contribute to the image-making of modern man. For in a true sense a person becomes what he thinks he is. His behavior and his relationships are affected by changes in his self-image. Whenever he adopts a new image of himself, to a certain extent he makes himself a new man, for the image is part of his being. As a theme in Christian thought and spirituality, man's making of man is not entirely new. Seventy years ago Friedrich von Hügel forcefully adumbrated the same insight. "With God as supreme and absolute reality, the moral Person in the world, we have been created and are helped by Him, in such conditions and according to such laws, as are conducive to our making ourselves into moral agents of a particular (our) kind and degree. . . . He intends to help us only to make our own selves, and gives us to begin with our materials but not the results, and *never, at any time, in the materials practically the results already.*" Indeed von Hügel goes so far as to allow that even as regards man's experience of God himself, "He made us in order that in a sense we might make Him." For the personality of God, though it "decides *in fact* even our first instant of existence, [yet] *as a conception of our own* . . . must, it too, be conquered and again be reformed and reconquered by us, with and through the conquest of our own personality." [12]

John Macquarrie has said that the Christian theologian must point beyond every reductive image to the image of self-transcendence in Christ who unveils all the mysterious potentialities of man. "The great task of the theologian, as it seems to me, will be to protect and enhance the mystery and transcendence of man—the deepest humanity of man. Sociology, psychology and similar sciences, as they have developed in America, have had as their presupposition a naturalistic view of man. . . . Theological anthropology will have its distinctiveness in exploring the truly human." [13] In the present collection this exploration has been done from several different points of view. The first three essays touch aspects of the human which in some way look to the future. The second three examine questions rooted more in the present. The last three deal with the thought of Pierre Teilhard de Chardin, to whom this writer owes an immense debt and who perhaps more than any other Christian thinker of the century was concerned with the making of man.

The notes to these essays make it clear how indebted the author is to the insights of others. Special gratitude, however, is due to Joseph P. Whelan, S.J., and Francis X. Winters, S.J., who read each essay and offered invaluable suggestions and criticism; to Mrs. Helen Zeccola for proofreading the entire manuscript; and to both her and Mrs. Bonnie Watters for typing the original material with their usual accuracy and good judgment. Selections from the following writings of Teilhard de Chardin are used with permission of Harper and Row, Publishers: *The Phenomenon of Man, The Divine Milieu, Writings in Time of War, The Vision of the Past, Letters from a Traveller, Science and Christ, The Making of a Mind, The Future of Man* and *Hymn of the Universe.*

PART ONE
A New Creation

I

Theology after the Council

The theme of what follows is that the significance of the Second Vatican Council for the future of theology is to be found in *Gaudium et Spes,* the Pastoral Constitution on the Church in the Modern World. This is not to say that the other documents are not also theologically very important, especially those dealing with the Church as a community, with revelation, worship and religious liberty. But their significance lies primarily in the present. What they have done, by and large, is to enable the Church to catch up theologically, to articulate that new consciousness of herself which she has developed in the twentieth century. The internal ecclesiological themes which are treated in these documents, those of collegiality, community, ecumenism, sacramental worship, authority of Scripture, freedom of conscience, etc., have all been the subjects of theological discussion for years, and what the Council did was simply to make its own the work theologians already had done. Nor do I wish to suggest that these subjects need no further development or theological precision. They do indeed, and the task of editing and interpreting conciliar texts must go on, as well as the corresponding task of rethinking the meaning and implications of what has been explicitly said. Again, such theology, however necessary, will not be primarily oriented toward the future; it rather concerns itself with consolidating the gains of the past and present, and protecting the lines of advance. It is precisely these lines of advance which concern us here, their presuppositions, their style, and their content, for their movement will tell us, not what the Church has been or is, but what she is likely to be.

Everyone who reads the Pastoral Constitution is conscious that

11

it touches the most fundamental problem of our time, namely, that of bridging the credibility gap between Christianity and modern man. Hence the importance of its fundamental assertion that both Church and world, however different the resources they can call upon, are seeking the same thing, namely how to make man succeed as man. The pivotal point, therefore, of what the Church can and must say to man today is man himself.[1] Never before has the Church officially proclaimed "by virtue of the Gospel committed to her . . . the rights of man." Never before has she publicly acknowledged that she "greatly esteems the dynamic movements of today by which these rights everywhere are fostered."[2] For the first time the Church has recognized the spirit of today's world. She wishes to "scrutinize the signs of the times" so as to interpret them in the light of revelation.[3] She explicitly acknowledges "the birth of a new humanism, one in which man is defined first of all by his responsibility toward his brothers and toward history."[4] Clearly the expectations and longings of modern man are of tremendous scope and diversity; his world one in which religion has only a tangential place. Yet it is with *this* man that the Church wishes to hold dialogue; it is *this* world which the Church wishes to help shape.

Now as Karl Rahner has said, this desire of the Church to find the man of today gives rise to far more radical questions than simply those which relate to a more realistic ecclesiology or to any of the other themes treated at length by the Council.[5] The Pastoral Constitution itself admits this: "Recent studies and findings of science, history and philosophy raise new questions affecting life and demanding new theological investigations. Furthermore, theologians are invited to seek continually, within the methods and requirements proper to theology, for more suitable ways of communicating doctrine to the men of their time; for the deposit of faith and revealed truths are one thing, the manner in which they are formulated without violence to their meaning and significance is another."[6] In what follows, then, I should like to deal briefly with three of the radical questions that theology will have to grapple with seriously if it wishes to communicate with modern man. They are all mentioned or at least alluded to in the Pastoral Constitution, for they all concern man in the world as the Church now encounters him.

I

The first question which challenges the future of theology is that of methodology. Before the Council it was presumed by the vast majority of Catholic systematic theologians that their discipline represented a recognized body of knowledge which could be passed on without ever taking into account the impact of change on human life. Yet the Pastoral Constitution begins with an exposition dealing precisely with the significance of this phenomenon of change. "Today's spiritual agitation and the changing conditions of life," it says, "are part of a broader and deeper revolution. As a result of the latter, intellectual formation is ever increasingly based on the mathematical and natural sciences and on those dealing with man himself, while in the practical order the technology which stems from these sciences takes on mounting importance. The scientific spirit exerts a new kind of impact on the cultural sphere and on modes of thought. . . . History itself speeds along at so rapid a course that an individual person can scarcely keep abreast of it. The destiny of the human community has become all of a piece, where once the various groups of men had a kind of private history of their own. Thus, the human race has passed from a rather static concept of reality to a more dynamic, evolutionary one, and the result is an immense series of new problems calling for new efforts of analysis and synthesis." [7]

This dynamic, evolutionary concept of reality cannot but profoundly affect the mood as well as the mode in which theology is done. The mood will be affected insofar as a theologian's attitude toward data is affected. To what extent are the data of revelation firm and given and to what extent are they to be searched for? Only in the last few years have Catholic theologians taken seriously the fact that the primary characteristic of revelation is its historicity. God reveals himself in and through history, and the truth of this revelation, while containing what is timeless, is nonetheless bound to a given time and culture. This means that one's understanding of a given truth can change radically, not superficially, with change in man's knowledge of himself and his world. Our present understanding of infallibility, salvation outside the Church and natural law, to cite but three examples, is significantly different from the understanding of the past. Theologians cannot claim, therefore, that they already possess eternally valid answers to questions which are time-bound and which can be solved only by listening to history. Yves Congar has well said that until recently Catholic theology so overemphasized the transcendental aspects of revelation that it seemed to confirm Nietzsche's judgment that Christianity was a new kind of Platonism for the crowds. History and society, Congar adds, far from being accidental contributions to the development of Christian ideas, are rather the material substrata out of which transcendent truth develops.[8]

It is generally agreed today that the very complex problem of doctrinal development is going to be with us for a long time to come. But an absolutely essential condition for its resolution is that a sense of changing reality color the whole mood in which theology is done. This means that serious research must be made into the relationship of theology to modern philosophies and to the physical and social sciences. Moral theology has already recognized that it cannot make statements about the ethics of sex or family life, for example, without knowing what psychology says about the human person or sociology about the human community. And it is well known that the writers of the Pastoral Constitution relied heavily upon experts in the social sciences in reaching their own conclusions. Not yet fully recognized, however, is that theological understanding even of Christian doctrines can be reached only in the context of what other disciplines say about reality. It is now commonplace to insist that theology must move away from its isolation in the seminary and into a university atmosphere. But little will be thereby accomplished if theologians are convinced beforehand that such serious conversation with the academic world really cannot result in any genuine development of doctrine, that is to say, a growth by which a quite new insight into meaning is possible. We are in fact experiencing the beginnings of such a growth in the area of ecclesiology, but it has been painfully lacking in Christology, eschatology, and the doctrine of God. Yet openness to such genuine development is the only attitude capable of bringing Catholic theology through the present unsettling period of transition, during which fragmentary theologizing as yet shows no signs of leading to a new integration.

This change of mood in theology must inevitably affect also the mode by which it is done. Until now this mode has been dominantly Hellenic, preferring abstract problems to concrete, dealing with unchanging human natures rather than human experience, emphasizing the eternal and necessary over the temporary and the contingent. The evolutionary outlook of the Pastoral Constitution, however, with its emphasis upon the human and the social, must lead in the opposite direction, namely toward that dehellenization so strongly advocated today, which is a reversal of that process by which Greek categories of thought have come to be normative in articulating the Christian message. Nor will this be an easy task. Bernard Lonergan has pointed out that such dehellenization demands the most delicate discrimination if it is to be done responsibly and intelligently. "Catholic theology today has a tremendous task before it," he writes, "for there are real limitations to Hellenism that have to be transcended by modern culture and have yet to be successfully surmounted by Catholic theology. But the task is not helped, rather it is gravely impeded, by wild statements based on misconceptions or suggesting unbelief." [9] This last statement means of course that there is real risk involved in trying to incarnate the Christian message into contemporary language and culture: essential Christian truths may get distorted or lost in the process of making them comprehensible and relevant. Yet this risk is the price we now have to pay for having desemitized Christianity. The major efforts now being made to articulate biblical affirmations in the more concrete Hebraic categories of time and action are attempts to recover thought forms which have been lost to the Western mind for centuries. This will not be done overnight and we shall have to put up in the meantime with that bewilderment and anxiety which characterize any truly human life in periods of radical change.

To conclude this discussion of methodology, we should note that the problem arises ultimately from the fact that the way a discipline is done in any given period depends upon how its practitioners feel in regard to their total body of knowledge. Since Vatican II, Catholic theologians generally feel they no longer have such a recognized body of knowledge. Thomism as a supporting philosophic structure for theology has in large measure collapsed and the very notion of a perennial philosophy would find few adherents today. Consequently it is not at all clear what is to be preserved, what abandoned, what transformed. The resulting orientation is rather toward the discovery of truth than toward its preservation, and hence toward original, creative theologizing rather than toward repetition of what has already been said. Any arbitrary standardization, therefore, which cannot gain support from the theological community, will immediately tend to be rejected or at best ignored. This community will be a pluralistic one, where no view will go unchallenged yet where each view will be respected for its integrity. In this atmosphere it will obviously be no small achievement for the Church to protect her unity. But this she can do precisely by promoting a plurality of theologies, none of which has a monopoly of truth, and by encouraging theologians to speak on many different levels. For by so doing she will show her trust in the judgments of the theological community as such, at the same time manifesting her true catholicity, her honesty and her acceptance of a world where cultural and intellectual pluralism are the order of the day.[10]

II

The challenge to theological methodology arising from the Council's recognition of historical change leads us now to consider the challenge of subject matter which has also come from the Council. The Pastoral Constitution suggests that two problem areas ought to move to the center of future theological concern. The first is the relationship between the Christian doctrine of God and the contemporary phenomenon of atheism. In fact it has been argued that the primary task of theology today is to awaken the Church to the seriousness of this question of atheism and to help Christians overcome this temptation in themselves. This it will do by integrating into its own reflection upon the Word of God that human questioning and doubt of which atheism is one logical interpretation. "Freedom in the process of evolving a logical atheism, and yet not ceasing to be challenged by God— that is the principal object of present theological research. . . . Not that the theologian wishes to reconcile conceptually the questioning of the atheist and the Word of God; rather he wants to go to the extreme of human questioning because the divine challenge erupts precisely where the spirit of man is on the move." [11]

What is at stake here is a recognition not only that the Christian doctrine of God is destined to undergo radical reevaluation, but also that theologians involved in such rethinking must accept as part of their own professional outlook that duality experienced by all thoughtful Christians today between their belief in God and their experience of his absence in modern life. The Pastoral Constitution asserts quite categorically that Christians themselves are partly to blame for the general increase of atheism, insofar as they have obscured or distorted God's image or failed to make the living God sufficiently visible in their lives.[12] Before the concept of God can be purified, therefore, it is necessary for theology to examine in far greater depth than heretofore the seeds of indifference and unbelief rooted in the heart of every believer. The "witness of a living and mature faith" called for by the Constitution must "prove its fruitfulness by penetrating the believer's entire life, including its worldly dimensions." [13] It must witness to a personal struggle for faith and an effort to overcome its ambiguity rather than be a recital of traditional argumentation. For it is in this struggle to conquer one's own temptation to unbelief that belief itself is brought to maturity.

The phenomenon of atheism must, then, in the dialectical process we are involved in, be used to deepen our understanding of the doctrine of God. Much of the rebellion today against Christian theism is against an absolutistic stereotype, and it is shared by Protestants and Catholics alike. Gabriel Marcel has said that we "have to be done with the idea of God as Cause, of a god concentrating in himself all causality, or even, in more rigorous terms, with all the theological usage of the notion of causality." And he adds that it could well be "that the God whose death Nietzsche truthfully announced was the god of the Aristotelian-Thomistic tradition, god the prime mover." [14] The "death of God" movement has in fact served to underline for most Catholic theologians the urgent need to shift the whole question of God to a much wider philosophical base than it has had in traditional Catholic theology. This means that Catholic theology must in the future become much more at home with contemporary secular philosophies. Protestant theologians have already done this, and are now strongly influenced in their speculations by process philosophy, existentialism, and to some extent by linguistic analysis. They seem, moreover, to be in general agreement in rejecting any concept of God as the unchanging absolute. While most Catholic theologians will not follow them this far, it is at least clear that both groups are now in a position to recognize the same problems.

The fundamental difficulty here is, of course, that the theologian has to talk about God as the ontological reality upon which Christian faith rests, and as yet there is no common agreement on how he is to do this if he begins, as he must today, with concrete phenomena and human experience. The greatest advance in this area may indeed be made by Bernard Lonergan, through his investigation of the relationship between human understanding and the methods of modern science. For he now believes theology to be approaching more and more an empirical science, in the sense that Scripture and tradition now supply it not with premises but with data, which in turn have to be interpreted in the light of contemporary techniques and procedures. The result is not demonstration and certitude but at best probability, with the discovery of new data leading to new hypotheses and more comprehensive judgments. The single constant in the operations of this empirical theology is reflection upon the concrete faith experience of conversion. For "when conversion is viewed as an ongoing process, at once personal, communal and historical, it coincides with living religion," and "empirical theology today is reflection upon religion." [15] This shift of foundation from objective theological statements to the experience of the thinking subject making such statements can provide a wholly new ground for speaking about God as ontological reality, while at the same time being faithful to the experience which men have of God at any given time in history.

It will readily be seen, from this approach of Lonergan, that the challenge of modern atheism is not simply a challenge to doctrine but also to spirituality; it forces us to rethink not only our concept of God but also our personal relationship to him. This double challenge is now being accepted by all Christian theologians, but perhaps no single person better symbolizes such acceptance than Pierre Teilhard de Chardin. More than one commentator has pointed out that it was under his influence that the full dimensions of the problem were recognized so clearly in the Pastoral Constitution. The style of prayer which developed in his own life was in fact an outgrowth of his desire to have a genuine experience of God in the midst of a world where God was thought irrelevant. The source of this experience he felt must be the divine presence and action at the heart of man's efforts to build the earth. This is why his frequent treatment of the theme of God's presence is of a piece with his efforts to rethink within an evolutionary world view the meaning of God's existence.[16] For in the case of modern man, it is only within such a world view, focused upon the future and upon man's achievement as man, that God can be spoken about or encountered in adoration and prayer. And here Teilhard faced a problem which he himself was not equipped to deal with as a theologian, but which is being rethought today in the writings of Johannes Metz, Wolfhart Pannenberg and Jürgen Moltmann, namely the relationship between secular eschatology and the theology of Christian hope.

It is very significant that the treatment of eschatology in the Pastoral Constitution is so closely linked with man's activity in the world. This eschatology is centered more upon humanity as a whole than upon the individual, more upon man's horizontal movement forward in time than upon his vertical orientation outside time. It is thus an effort to show that Christianity is not powerless in face of the predominance of the future in the modern mind. "The expectation of a new earth," the Constitution says, "must not weaken but rather stimulate our concern for cultivating this one. For here grows the body of a new human family, a body which even now is able to give some kind of foreshadowing of the new age. . . . To the extent that [earthly progress] can contribute to the better ordering of human society, it is of vital concern to the kingdom of God." [17] Thus God's Spirit not only "arouses a desire for the age to come, but, by that very fact, he animates, purifies and strengthens those noble longings too by which the human family strives to make its life more human and to render the whole earth submissive to this goal." This same Spirit, continues the text, frees men to put aside love of self, to bring "all earthly resources into the service of human life," and to "devote themselves to that future when humanity itself will become an offering accepted by God." [18]

Now the eschatology sketched here by the Council in its barest outline is one which deals with what is most central in the life of twentieth-century man, his hopes for the future. As such it confronts the chief dynamism in the contemporary denial of God's presence, namely an optimism based upon man's sense of autonomy and his conviction that he is master of his own destiny. As such also it provides a counterdynamism actually to find God in the world, namely an assertion that God is present precisely in the future that man is now making, that God will meet him there each day at that point where human action is most creative. In this perspective the experience of God's transcendence begins with an experience of a future toward which man is always moving, but which is never fully realized and so ever beyond his reach.[19] Hence the significance of the social concern of the Pastoral Constitution, its clear directives regarding man's responsibility for his fellow man in justice and love. Man will find God and experience him precisely by involvement in the economic and political life of our time, in its struggle for peace and its efforts to build a new world culture and a community for all men.

This question of God's existence and our experience of him is intimately connected, then, with our involvement in the hopes and aspirations of mankind. Such human hope is a reflection and a correlative of the constant affirmation of Scripture that God is always faithful to his promises. What prevents this hope from becoming a mere utopian daydream is precisely our knowledge that the God of Exodus and resurrection is the God of hope, and that the future has in fact already come in Christ. This is why the Pastoral Constitution can be so genuinely optimistic, while clearly recognizing the disruptive power of evil whereby vanity and malice can transform human energies into sin.[20] The Christian can bear with this because he finds in God alone the power of a future that must bring not destruction but fulfillment. The emerging theology of hope is thus both a theology of resurrection and a theology of history. "Where God proclaims his presence, the God-forsakenness of the world turns into suffering," says Jürgen Moltmann. "We begin to suffer from the conditions of our world, if we begin to love the world. And we begin to love the world if we are able to discover hope for it. And we discover hope for this world, if we hear the promise of a future which stands against frustration, transiency and death. . . . To be sure, we can hope for God only in the pain of an open theodicy question." [21]

III

Thus far we have been discussing the first problem area which must move to the center of future theological concern as a result of the Council, namely the relationship between the Christian doctrine of God and the contemporary phenomenon of atheism. The second problem area is no less important and is very closely connected with the first: the relationship between Christology and the new humanism of post-modern man. Before the Council the more common conviction was that Christianity was primarily concerned with man's worship of God in and through Christ. Its thrust was contemplative, therefore, and stressed an orientation away from the world rather than toward it. The theology which became dominant at the Council, however, holds that Christianity is concerned primarily with the humanization of man and his transformation in Christ. Theology must therefore "not only reflect on revelation but also it has somehow to mediate God's meaning into the whole of human affairs." [22] This mediation, moreover, can only take place within a Christology, that is to say, within an effort to articulate the significance of the relationship of divine to human as these exist in the Person of Christ. Everything human must somehow find its fulfillment in the humanity of the incarnate Word, for in assuming human nature Christ showed forth the ultimate plan of God for all human values; while remaining human, they are destined to transcend themselves through the action of God.

The single theme running through the whole of the Pastoral Constitution is precisely this effort to reflect upon the mystery of salvation brought by Christ in terms of a humanization as well as of a divinization of man. Christ "entered the world's history as a perfect man, taking that history up into himself and summarizing it," and is now "at work in the hearts of men through the energy of the Spirit." [23] And in another passage it states that "only in the mystery of the incarnate Word does the mystery of man take on light." He it is who "fully reveals man to man himself . . . for by his Incarnation the Son of God has united himself in some fashion to every man. . . . All this holds true not only for Christians, but for all men of good will in whose hearts grace works in an unseen way." [24] Finally, "though the same God is Savior and Creator, Lord of human history as well as of salvation history, in the divine arrangement itself the rightful autonomy of the creature, and particularly of man, is not withdrawn. Rather it is reestablished in its own dignity and strengthened in it." [25]

Now the Christological thrust of these statements focuses attention upon two interlocking areas which must be seriously rethought by theologians in the years to come: the relationship of Christ's work of redemption to the whole cosmic reality, and man's consequent need of grace in those aspects of his life most specifically human and secular. Certainly the impression has been created in the past that the Christian message was one of salvation *from* the world, that revelation had very little to say about the meaning of the secular, and that what man accomplished in his building of the earthly city was little touched by the action of God. This impression was deepened by manuals of theology in which both grace and redemption were considered exclusively as matters involving God and the soul alone, and where the death and resurrection of Christ were treated as something quite unrelated to the work of creation. This, however, is no longer possible. The identity of the Person of the Word with both the God who created and the Christ who redeemed has led to a conviction now that the two works are not distinct but form a single whole. Many theologians today, both those who follow the lead of Teilhard de Chardin and those who work independently of him, wish indeed to give the Incarnation a cosmic scope, but at the same time they want to show how in his cosmic role Christ in fact fulfills his salvific role. Christ is thus the God of creation insofar as he is its Savior. In this sense the total mystery of Christ is redemptive insofar as it constitutes a *kenosis* into matter involving a necessary participation in that suffering and death common to all men. The healing of the wound of sin by restoration of God's friendship must therefore be seen as a freeing of man to be more fully man, and no theology of original sin will be acceptable in the future which does not link it with the human condition separated from Christ in which man is unable to be fully himself.[26]

It will be clear from what has been said that any future developments in the doctrine of grace must deal with the relationship of the profane and secular to God precisely as profane and secular. Christ's work of salvation cannot be limited to what has traditionally been called the sphere of "religion," for to Christianize the profane must mean, not to make it any less profane, but to help it become more completely itself. The theological problem here is twofold: first, to spell out the ontological priority of grace by which the world has become Christic independently of contact with institutional Christianity; second, to establish the precise relationship between humanity as the whole people of God and the Church as the Body of Christ. Christians today do not want to involve themselves in anything which separates them from the mainstream of human life. They want their Church to embrace the whole of mankind, as the Pastoral

Constitution clearly intends. They want the world and the Church to move toward Christ not in parallel lines but by an interpenetration, an osmosis as Edward Schillebeeckx has called it, so that while the Church keeps her sense of identity as the Body of Christ, the boundaries between herself and the world become permanently blurred. Blurred too as a consequence would be distinctions between sacred and secular, religious and profane. To be credible today, the Church cannot stand apart from the world any more than Christ did through the Incarnation; nor can creation ever be considered alone, complete in itself, independently of its elevation through grace.[27]

A further Christological problem opened up by what has been said thus far is that of the autonomy of secular activity. On the one hand, the human activity of Christ cannot be thought to be any less autonomous as human activity by reason of its being under the control of the Person of the Word. This is the basis for the Pastoral Constitution's insistence upon the rightful independence of earthly affairs. "If by the autonomy of earthly affairs we mean that created things and societies themselves enjoy their own laws and values which must be gradually deciphered, put to use and regulated by men, then it is entirely right to demand that autonomy. . . . For by the very circumstance of their being created, all things are endowed with their own stability, truth, goodness, proper laws, and order." [28] On the other hand, however, contemporary man's unprecedented awareness of his autonomy is precisely what has dulled his sense of dependence upon God and of the transcendent aspect of ordinary human life. Needed, therefore, is a theological anthropology in which all the humanistic endeavor of man would retain autonomy in its own sphere, yet never be seen as an absolute, independent of God's initiative and freedom. The role of grace would thus be to keep men open to this action of God at the heart of the process whereby man grows in his humanity. No humanism can become an idol if the men embracing it see it as their cooperation with God in the development of man. Man's experience of his own freedom and creative initiative would thus at the same time be an experience of the transcendent action of God.

Finally, the relationship between Christology and the new humanism will never be satisfactorily articulated in the future unless very serious consideration is given to the impact of non-Christian religious thought upon the changing culture of man. The Pastoral Constitution says explicitly that "the circumstances of the life of modern man have been so profoundly changed in their social and cultural aspect that we can speak of a new age of human history." The speed of communication "opens more widely to all the treasures of different civilizations and thus, little by little, there develops a more universal form of human culture which better promotes and expresses the unity of the human race." [29] In the face of an emerging world culture, then, the attitude of the Church is clearly one of openness. "Sent to all peoples of every time and place, [the Church] is not bound exclusively . . . to any particular way of life. . . . Faithful to her own tradition and at the same time conscious of her universal mission, she can enter into various civilizations." [30] On the level of theology, however, relatively little has been done to evaluate the place of the great world religions in God's plan of salvation in Christ. As a result the base of the Christian theology has been too narrow for it to speak meaningfully to the modern mind oriented toward the planetary unification of man. A Christology which in any way alienates the Christian from the totality of man's religious experience, both of the past and of the future, will simply not be meaningful. The Christian today is in search of a world identity. He wants to know what his faith in Christ means when he confronts the still unanswered question of the presence of God's redemptive action in the hearts of his non-Christian brothers. It is in this context that the mission of the Church as Body of Christ must be rethought. Such rethinking may well receive its greatest impetus from dialogue already begun with Judaism, that religion within which the Church took her origin and along with which she shares a common destiny. A deeper understanding of Christ's relationship to the Jewish people could well be, in God's providence, the beginning of a Christology better related to any emerging humanism for the whole world.

IV

The theme of this chapter has been that the Second Vatican Council, through its Pastoral Constitution on the Church in the Modern World, has underlined the importance of three areas likely to make the greatest demands upon future theological research, namely those of methodology, Christology and the doctrine of God. Underlying our discussion has been the conviction, voiced many times by Bernard Lonergan, that the crisis we are now experiencing in theology is not one of faith but one of culture. The present breaking down of classical culture means the breakdown too of that theology whose thought forms depend upon it. "Classical culture cannot be jettisoned without being replaced," Lonergan writes, "and what replaces it cannot but run counter to classical expectations. There is bound to be formed a solid right that is determined to live in a world that no longer exists. There is bound to be formed a scattered left, captivated by now this, now that new development. . . . But what will count is perhaps a not numerous center, big enough to be at home in both the old and the new, painstaking enough to work out one by one the transitions to be made, strong enough to refuse half-measures and insist on complete solutions even though it has to wait." [31] All would agree, I think, that patient waiting must certainly characterize theologizing in the immediate future. This means, first of all, that theologians themselves must be attentive to the world now developing around them, for the more they understand how they think in the present, the better will they understand why they think as they do about both the past and the future. "Christian theology is improperly done," says Julian Hartt, "when it comes only at the end . . . to consider the cultural situation of faith. . . . Theology proper must begin with the analysis of culture, or it will prove to be systematically meaningless." [32]

But a theology characterized by patient waiting must also recognize that there has appeared both during and after the Council a disconcerting lack of communication between the center and the periphery of the Catholic Church. What has become evident is that the style of doing theology at the periphery is very different from the style at the center. Catholic theology has thus become unsettled because the Church herself has become unsettled. Fragmentation is therefore inevitable and should be a source not of insecurity but of hope. On condition, of course, that confidence is shown to all theologians, even to those on the periphery whose conclusions do not agree with the Roman outlook. Otherwise there will be no chance of retaining that degree of tension necessary both for equilibrium and for the reassessment of doctrinal development. It is easy to state, for example, as does the Roman center, that Christian revelation is concerned with more than building the earthly city. But this does little to answer the pressing question on the periphery which asks what building the earthly city has to do with Christian revelation. What is needed, then, is not a dissolution of conflict but rather a realization that its existence between center and periphery is a healthy manifestation of that tension between transcendence and immanence which characterizes the Christian life as a whole. The remarks of Edward Schillebeeckx in this regard provide a fitting close. "Just as the harmonious relationship between the natural and supernatural is, at the moral level of human life, not a 'datum,' but a task full of conflicts and risks, so too does the harmonious relationship between the impulse toward incarnation and disincarnation, at the level of theological thought, only come about dramatically in conflicts and polemics. . . . Throughout history, therefore, theology is always passing through a crisis of growth, as a result of which its true face is always appearing in a purer form." [33]

II

Prayer, Time and Hope

Over a decade ago Romano Guardini spoke of the disenchantment that could come to the life of prayer with the widespread realization that most of what we experience in the world is the direct effect either of the natural operation of things themselves or of their manipulation by man. Such a tendency to judge everything from the point of view of ascertainable laws would eventually rob our lives of mystery and our awareness of God's presence of an essential support. For a sense of mystery and presence is conditioned by a sense of divine activity; if the latter is diminished, then prayer, which is the spontaneous reaction to mystery and presence, must inevitably be diminished too. Guardini insists, however, that this can only happen if God's activity in the universe, his "physical" presence, is thought of somehow as impersonal, divorced from that freedom and initiative which have always marked his interventions into human life. "All cosmic processes, all phenomena and events to which our sensory perception and intellect give us access, occur within a system of laws. . . . But the system as such is but an instrument in the hands of God's creative freedom; at the same time it is an expression and proof of the consistency with which this freedom works. Thus everything that happens, everything which is, has the character of a gift-of-grace and must be included in our thanksgiving." [1]

The contemporary malaise in prayer, however, which Guardini saw being fostered primarily by modern science, has been immeasurably intensified by recent developments in theology, especially the "death of God" phenomenon and the growth of "religionless" Christianity. These and other movements have turned

28

our current approach to the God question into a genuine search. We are more keenly aware perhaps than any previous generation that we may have been speaking about and praying to an idol rather than the true God. We want now desperately to find him, to become aware of his presence in the most personal way, and we are quite willing to admit with Guardini that we have neglected the element of mystery. Yet this element will not soon be reinstated in its rightful place either in theology or in prayer. We have analyzed too long, dissected concepts and evaluated data too carefully, to welcome now an admission that the God we adore is indeed a God we cannot know. At the same time we must recognize that the aim of any sound theology is not to dissolve mystery but to locate it, to push the mind as far as it will go into that darkness which is boundless light. The theologian's task is fulfilled precisely when he is able at the end of his quest to know that he does not know, and to lapse into the silence of reverence. "We cannot," wrote Thomas Aquinas, "contemplate how God is but only how he is not." [2] And again: "The ultimate in human knowledge of God is to know that we do not know him." [3]

There are, nevertheless, two approaches to the personal and the mysterious in our relations with God which may be of help for prayer. One concerns the role played by time in Christian life, the other the role played by hope. Both approaches accordingly involve concern for the future and the "not yet," and underline the fact that today the eschatological ought to characterize our prayer as much as it already does our theology. Indeed, we should naturally expect all prayer to be some form of expectation, since by definition it is the growing point of our encounter with God. Let us see, then, to what extent the personal and the mysterious can be illumined when prayer is seen first in the context of time and then in the context of Christian hope.

I

Among the many beneficial effects which modern biblical scholarship has had on Christian spirituality, not the least has been the rediscovery of the Hebraic sense of time. The concrete and personalized time of the Hebrews may not be capable of solving some time problems in modern philosophy, but for the Christian it has provided a framework within which he can more clearly recognize his spiritual life for the historical process it is. In contrast to the static categories of the Greeks and of Western thought in general, reality for the Hebrews was a movement, a movement personally directed by God, who through his active intervention into human life led both individual and community toward a specific goal. Consequently, the Hebrews and early Christians found it quite easy to think of their relationship with God precisely as a history, as an engagement in a series of historical events over which God was always the Lord.

Initially, therefore, the Christian experience was more one of becoming than of being. Though both experiences are necessary in order to grasp reality in its wholeness, the fact is that most spiritual writers in the West, at least since the fifteenth century, have followed the scholastic theologians and avoided the dynamic element in man's relationship with God. A case in point is the biblical description of what we now call sanctifying grace. To be a "son of God" and "temple of the Holy Spirit" meant, for many centuries, to have a living awareness through faith of a new affective orientation toward the three divine Persons as well as a participation in their sanctifying activity. The union of all Christians as members of Christ's Body was likewise thought of in terms of the same dynamic relationship effected through the action of the Holy Spirit. The scholastic concern for abstract natures, however, led to a static concept of grace as a special participation in the divine nature through the reception of a created gift, seen now as an "accident" inhering in the soul. Christians were united to each other because they all possessed this created gift, although the social aspect of grace was seldom insisted upon. While preserving all that is valuable in this point of view, theologians today have returned to the concept of grace as a communion between persons. Chiefly emphasized is the indwelling and friendship of the three Persons, which constitutes a new mode of existence for the Christian rather than a new nature. Members of Christ's Body prolong in their turn this divine activity within them by living sacramental lives; that is to say, by entering into the thoughts and actions of Christ and so thinking and acting as he would in their circumstances.

Now this theological stress upon human existence in the concrete, coupled with the biblical stress upon reality as movement, can have a significant influence upon one's prayer. The Christian vocation will present itself, from this point of view, as a call to play a specific role in the forward movement of salvation history between the first and second comings of Christ. My own point of time thus becomes extremely important, for it is at this point that I am caught up into that continual re-creation in Christ which is God's ultimate purpose in the paschal mystery, and which in fact constitutes the presence of the paschal mystery in the past, present and future of my life. The special significance of my personal call by God is that the paschal mystery is to be reenacted in the world through me. By reason of his birth at a certain point in time, Christ's immediate influence on earth was limited: he became a Jew, to live and die in a particular cultural milieu, bounded by the geography of a land and the mentality of a people. Only through the individual Christian can Christ become incarnate in other cultures, and only through me can he become incarnate in the specific area in which I make my presence felt. To be a Christian, therefore, means first of all that I do not face my world unwillingly, but accept that place in time which God has allotted to me.

Yet my following of Christ also means a readiness to accept a future whose nature and circumstances I cannot now foresee. The apostles knew practically nothing of what Christ expected of them; they knew only that they wanted to be with him and they were content to leave their future in his hands. Unless I too am prepared for the unforeseen and the unexpected, I may not be able to recognize the bridegroom when he comes in the middle of the night. This readiness to commit oneself to a future more or less unknown is in fact a characteristic of all love. He who loves, writes Karl Rahner, "must start out *today* on the adventure of a love which not until tomorrow will be what it should be tomorrow. . . . Love today is what it should be today only if it acknowledges today that it is something of which more will be demanded tomorrow. Love is true love even for today only if it strives to become more than it is today, only if it is truly in movement, reaching out for what lies ahead of it." [4]

Our mode of union with Christ will thus correspond to our growing and changing awareness of the reality which is ourselves and of those historical events which give our lives their structure. Each of our experiences must be seen with the eye of faith as an experience of God's presence, revealing to us what he wishes our lives to become. Commitment to Christ does not mean following a blueprint or adhering to a timetable; it means listening to the voice of God and accepting the gift which he offers. Though God's choice is eternal, it must be ratified by a response in time, and this can be made only gradually, over the whole course of our lives. Hence the need on our part of vigilance. "Be on the alert at every moment, praying to come safely through all that lies before you and for the meeting with the Son of Man." [5] These words of Christ are echoed by St. John: "Here and now we are God's children; what we shall be has not yet been disclosed." [6] Such disclosure will come at God's appointed time, and it is this which forbids our making beforehand any autonomous plan of our own. Our movement toward the future must always be provisional, since it is a movement into the unknown. Ultimately this movement is a mystery, for the God who governs our lives is himself a mystery.

There is, however, a light for us to follow, and it comes from a source we should least expect: our past. In the Old Testament, Yahweh made it clear that the Israelites were to carry their past with them always, for it was their past, that series of great divine interventions in their lives, which made them different from all other nations and peoples. So he constantly reminded them that he was their God, that he had led them out of Egypt, across the Red Sea and through the desert, and that it was he who had finally brought them to the promised land.[7] Only by remembering their past could the Israelites be faithful when the Word of God came to them again in their present. Indeed, the whole drama and tragedy of God's dealings with his people revolve around their forgetfulness. The preaching of the prophets is one long reminder that misfortunes and trials are meant to be occasions for remembering once more what God had already done for them. Such recollection was to become Israel's pledge of liberation and to constitute its hope of future glory.[8]

In the New Testament, on a somewhat deeper level, we are reminded that our recollection of God's past generosity can be transformed into an awareness of what he is actually accomplishing in the present. For in the Person of Christ, who sums up all history in himself, we have the continual accomplishment of all God's promises to the world. "He is the Yes pronounced upon God's promises, every one of them." [9] In Christ mankind is effectively present to God and God to mankind. Through Christ we too become present to God and God to us. This is why the work of his Spirit in the life of the Christian is to "make everything plain and recall to your minds whatever I have said to you." [10] Such an experience we have above all through the Eucharist, which is the re-presentation of the Pasch and therefore a re-presentation also of all that God has ever done in any human life.

This light from the past, coming to us in the present, brings with it further insights. "To be" is now seen to mean in a very true sense "to be receiving." "What do you possess that you have not received?" [11] We are all in danger of shutting ourselves up in the "now" of our relationship with God, as though the past were something with no influence any more, and the future nothing but a repetition of the present. Whereas it is precisely the past which reveals the meaning of our mysterious "now," and so nourishes our hope by bearing witness to the generosity of God. The doctrine of merit is not unrelated to this: everything good we have done in our past remains in our present and is operative both in our union with God and in our work for our neighbor. Only the evil we have done disappears. And even in the case of evil action, there are good effects on the human plane which will persist and await their own turn to be glorified. Thus what we are continually receiving from God is a redemption of time itself. What we have to look forward to is not simply the resurrection of our bodies but a resurrection as well of time into eternity.

At this point we come upon the startling paradox of the Christian life. Union with God can be understood only in its past accomplishment, it can be lived only in its present reality, but it can be fully possessed only in its future achievement. This is the primary meaning of the eschatological tendency in the lives of the first Christians, their anticipation of the "Not Yet," their preoccupation with the Parousia of Christ, which many of us find strange and sometimes perplexing. Their remembrance of the past somehow tended more and more to be transformed into expectation. Hidden in this experience is the profound truth that our past has no real significance outside the future to which God has destined us; and, conversely, that preoccupation with our future can become a dangerous daydream unless our movement toward it is based upon the acceptance of our present and past. Each Christian, in other words, needs time not only to develop the rhythm of his life with God, but even more to discover it. To be related to Christ in faith, hope, and charity indeed means to be in a "state" of union, but even more it means to be involved in a certain rhythm of growth. Such an understanding of Christian expectation can provide a new and realistic context for the classic formula which says that in the spiritual life we either progress or fall back, but there is no standing still.

From this point of view it can readily be seen why the Christian in the modern world should have a double orientation toward the future. He must be aware, first of all, that his own spiritual development as a person is an integral part of a time process involving the development of the human race as a whole. The forces at work for millions of years in the evolutionary process did not suddenly cease to operate when man arrived on the scene. This means not simply that they continue now in man; it means also, and more importantly, that the whole process is being carried out by man. He is indeed lord of the earth.[12] It is he who invents and discovers and who has, by taking into his own hands the direction of the world, gradually replaced nature in the progress of life. Upon man, therefore, falls the awful responsibility for his future on earth; but it is a future inextricably connected with the second coming of Christ. All human activity which is motivated by Christ's charity shoulders this human responsibility in a special way. It is a participation in God's own creative activity, and therefore serves to build up the whole Body of

Christ.[13] A man's spiritual growth is thus inseparable from the growth of the universe into which he has been born. As we have noted already, the Christian awaits not the future imposition of a pre-existent scheme, but rather the mysterious involvement of his own free decisions in the free decisions of God. These free decisions regarding one's personal spiritual development are actually related to those of the human race as a whole, and by this very fact related also to the second coming of Christ at the end of time.

At this point it would not be out of place to underline once again the single idea we have been developing, namely that if one's relationship to God is to be authentic it must be an engagement with history. This means first of all one's own history. Our attitude toward prayer changes and indeed must change. The gift which we bring to him over the years is not the same gift, and hence our mode of offering it cannot be the same. Fundamentally this is because we ourselves are different. If spiritual development means anything, it means that the seed must die before it can bring forth fruit. In the course of time, through God's action on our souls and the events that shape our lives, we die a little to our selfish interests and thereby allow Christ to live a little more in us. Moreover, as the years pass we see with greater clarity what the gift of ourselves to God really means; and this new knowledge affects both the work we do for him and the whole range of our personal relationships. That we should gradually come of age spiritually and find new forms in which to express ourselves is both natural and to be expected. Time is thus not an enemy but a friend. Changes taking place in us on the human level will always have their counterpart in changes on the level of grace. St. Paul's words are meant to describe both types of growth: "When I was a child my speech, my outlook, my thoughts were all childish. When I grew up, I had finished with childish things." [14]

Nevertheless, our engagement with history implies more than this. For the precise way in which we change cannot but be conditioned by the way the world is changing. Mankind as a whole is growing to maturity, and to the extent that we are involved in the mainstream of human life we shall influence and be influenced by this growth. This implies a willingness on the part of the Christian to bring into greater harmony his own desire to come close to Christ and the desire of modern man to develop and conquer the earth. More than one observer has noted that there exists in the minds of most Christians today a conceptual gap between being holy and being human, between commitment to the eternal and commitment to the temporal, between loving God and loving the world. Bishop Robinson's *Honest to God* has given eloquent witness to this growing inability, even of sincere Christians, to resolve this dichotomy or to find any relevance for their lives in religious orientations which are extra-temporal. Christian spirituality cannot ignore this problem under pain of becoming relevant. It must be faced, if not willingly then at least honestly and with courage.

It is therefore dangerous to speak of growth in sanctity today without speaking at the same time of the contribution which such growth makes toward the great human aspirations of man. This is not in any sense to impoverish man's quest for God by presenting its goal of divine union as some materialistic utopian dream. It is simply to recognize that the most startling manifestation of the divine transcendence is precisely God's presence in the world, first in the heart of man and then in the creative impetus behind every truly human achievement. "The glory of God is man fully alive," said Irenaeus. The sense of time and movement of which we have spoken is at its deepest level a sense of God; and to develop the one is to add depth to the other. The past, present and future of our relations with God are not in fact the idyllic dialogue which some would have us believe. For in point of fact, no change takes place in our relationship with God without repercussions in the lives of those around us, and hence without an increasing influence upon the world at large. The comings of Christ to each of us in succeeding moments of time are indeed meant to prepare for his final coming in our resurrection at the end of time. But this final coming is also destined to crown man's efforts to shape his world and to transform the world he has shaped. The Christian who looks forward to the Parousia as the ultimate fulfillment of God's plan for his life must recognize, then, that in this culmination of salvation there is also to be found the ultimate fulfillment of all man's human hopes, all of his obscure human faith in the triumph of life over death.

II

Up to now we have been discussing the influence of time and history upon one's sense of prayer, and we have alluded frequently to the eschatological tendency in the lives of the early Christians. Their preoccupation with the future, however, was always an anticipation of God's coming to man, and so was inextricably connected with both the personal and the mysterious. Prayer for them was simply an expression of hope. I think we can say that in the common Christian consciousness today this hope has three aspects and it will be helpful now to disengage these and to underline their significance for our current approach to prayer.

The first aspect of Christian hope, and the one which has perhaps the greatest influence on prayer, is the recognition that the personal activity of God touches the very center of human life. While the average Christian would not dream of holding, as Pelagius did, that man can attain his destiny by his own natural efforts, he tends to take it for granted that in reaching out for that destiny man is somehow autonomous and alone. The Church, on the other hand, has always insisted that man can initiate nothing in regard to his ultimate happiness. If he freely reaches out toward God, it must be God who first moves him. In no sense does man save himself. The biblical doctrine of election means that salvation comes as a pure gift through Christ from the strong hands of God. Throughout the Old and New Testaments man is seen as being continually drawn into co-activity with God, and Christian faith is presented precisely as an instruction in this sacred history and a call to understand and take part in it.

For many a Christian this involves an insuperable problem in regard to man's freedom only because he has come to think of freedom as necessarily equated with autonomy. In this he is a creature of his time. Autonomy and self-sufficiency have come to be revered as absolutes. Dietrich von Hildebrand has noted that modern man wants desperately to eliminate the element of surprise in his life. He wants to receive no gifts, but to determine everything himself, to claim everything as his right. He is no longer willing to admit that factor in his life as creature which is often called "chance" and which a Christian would call providence, but rather seeks to replace it with a human insurance policy against anything unforeseen. Ultimately this rebellion against his creatureliness reaches its own breaking point in the helplessness he feels when such human insurance fails, and factors beyond his control begin to multiply and close in upon him. For the autonomous man is not only self-sufficient, he is also alone. Loneliness and insecurity are just as characteristic of our present age as the desire for autonomy, and all three can be seen to a marked degree in many a Christian's life. Independence may dominate his exterior, but the thought which more and more preoccupies his mind is that tomorrow's horizon may be darkened by a mushroom cloud.

Autonomy is indeed man's prerogative in relation to created nature, to forms of life that are below him. But his movement toward God comes as an invitation to friendship on another plane of being, to a sharing in the intimate life of God which is the personal possession of Christ, the Father and the Spirit. That such a sharing should be man's final destiny and the whole purpose of his existence, is a mystery as deep and unfathomable as God himself. But what it means concretely for the individual is that any thought or desire he has, any decision he reaches, which is even remotely connected with bringing him closer to his final destiny, is a thought, a desire, a decision springing ultimately from a divine initiative at work in the depths of his soul. "Both the will to do it and the accomplishment of that will are something which God accomplishes in you, to carry out his loving purpose." [15] Man is free to reject this divine initiative, to refuse to be drawn into co-activity with God, but the price he pays is to involve himself in that terrible autonomous flight from his destiny called personal sin. It is impossible to have any understanding of sin at all unless it be seen not as a breaking of rules but as a refusal of friendship, as isolation from God. When such a refusal becomes eternally ratified, then it is hell, for hell is essentially the fulfillment of an ultimate and irrevocable desire to be completely independent, completely autonomous, completely alone.

We cannot ignore the implications of this mystery under pain of shutting ourselves up in unreality. Frank Sheed's example of the coat hanging on the wall is very much to the point. If a person's mind does not see a hook beneath the coat, it means he thinks the coat is hanging there by its own power, and that makes him wrong on the nature of coats, the nature of walls and the law of gravity. If failure to see so small a thing as a hook means a deranged universe, how much more the failure to recognize and take into account the most important element in a man's whole psychological makeup: the personal activity of God at the center of the human heart. To think that man is autonomous and alone in reaching decisions affecting his ultimate happiness, is to be wrong on the very nature of man, to see nothing in his life as it is and everything as it is not.

In this whole mysterious relationship between man's freedom and God's salvific grace, there is a central truth which we are tempted persistently to overlook: the source of all God's activity on the human soul is love. It is because we seldom advert to this that we tend to think of our freedom as somehow injured and restricted by grace, as if a divine initiative proceeding from love could ever hurt the delicate mechanism of man's freedom which God himself has created. Is man to be thought less free because he is enabled to transcend himself and to reach the destiny for which he was made? In directing the power of his love toward man, says Romano Guardini, God enables man's freedom to emerge in its fullest measure, with all its marvelous capacity to perfect the human personality. Whatever of eternal worth man is or is able to achieve has as its origin this single source. This union within the single human act of God's loving initiative and man's free response is a meshing as delicate as gossamer. It cannot be reduced to a mere intellectual problem. Ultimately it is an object not of probing curiosity but of reverence and adoration.

As a corollary to this first aspect of Christian hope, namely the recognition that God's personal activity touches the very center of human life, there appears a second, namely a pervasive sense of one's dependence upon God. For hope derives from faith in Christ as the full expression of God's will and activity, and thus depends upon the power of God to use our prayer to accomplish his own purpose. All prayer, therefore, is a form of expectation, an adherence in the present to that which we believe and hope will be realized in the future. Such anticipation is no compulsive figment of the imagination by which we pretend that things are not what they really are. Rather, as Peter Baelz has said, it is a contemplation of their present actuality within the context of the reality of the eternal purposes of God; a seeing of the world and our neighbor in the light of the new creation in Christ.[16] Because it looks forward to what God has still to do in and through those who respond to his love, such prayer will always have the aspect of petition and intercession. Petitionary prayer thus appears as that point at which God's providence and the Christian's faith coincide. It is simultaneously both passive and active, for its dependence upon God is dependence upon a love which enhances man's freedom rather than diminishing it, and dependence upon a power "able to do immeasurably more than all we ask or imagine." [17]

Yet it is extremely important to make clear what such dependence means. Much of the confusion regarding the relationship between prayer and hope can arise, as D. Z. Phillips has well observed, from misunderstanding what it means to say that with God all things are possible. Obviously God cannot do the logically impossible. But there is often another conviction: that prayer can in some way necessitate what is prayed for, that there is some *necessary* connection between what one hopes and prays for and what one receives. Whereas to see all things as possible in God must, in fact, mean seeing God alone as necessary and all future possibilities in our lives as merely possible. That is to say, no single one of these possibilities can really be necessary in order for us either to live or to be happy or to love God. Nor can we believe it necessary for any one of these possibilities actually to happen, for such would be the belief of a fatalist. Rather, as Phillips points out, "Praying to God for whom all things are possible, is to love God in *whatever* the case." [18] Prayer of petition is thus ultimately not an attempt to influence the way things go, so much as a request to be submissive to God *through* the way things go. It is an expression of hope to be delivered from any desires which may threaten our relationship to God. The dependence involved here is thus radically a dependence upon *God,* and not upon the prayer itself. Our hope is in God and not in the frequency or purity or intensity of our prayer. Søren Kierkegaard has written compellingly on this point and it will be worth quoting him at length:

> Inasmuch as for God all things are possible, it may be said that this is what God is, viz. one for whom all things are possible. The worship of the fatalist is therefore at its maximum an exclamation, and essentially it is dumbness, dumb submission; he is unable to pray. So to pray is to breathe, and possibility is for the self what oxygen is for breathing. . . . In order to pray there must be a God, there must be a self plus possibility . . . for God *is* that all things are possible, and that all things are possible *is* God. . . . The fact that God's will is the possible makes it possible for me to pray; if God's will is only the necessary, man is essentially as speechless as the brutes.[19]

The dependence on God of which we are speaking is likewise closely linked with the hope of delivery from guilt, since forgiveness of sin is in reality hope for oneself as a person. Here again the relation to faith and love is clear: only through faith does one see that to be truly free is to be saved from sin by Christ's love. This salvific intervention of God is alone capable of healing the interior division within man himself. Nothing that man can do by way of initiative or creativity is of any avail. Prayer and hope for forgiveness are thus the supreme admission of one's helplessness. They involve not simply an expression of grief and contrition but a request for a new outpouring of God's love, and it is this which the sinner has no right to expect. Faced with the cross of Christ he becomes vividly aware not only of what is awry in his own life, but of everything in the world that is evil and inhuman. The apprehension of God's salvific action in Jesus, while initially one of self-understanding and interior renewal, thus contains within itself a new vision both of history and of nature. Reflected in the reconciliation of the sinner is a love which will also transfigure the world. Hence hope for oneself as a person involves also hope for the world. The existential insight of dependence thus takes on a cosmic significance, and prayer for one's own healing becomes an anticipation of what is still to be revealed for mankind as a whole. "Dreams of the future," writes Jürgen Moltmann, "characteristically play down the value of the present. Man with his thoughts lives in a state of unreality which does not yet exist and which may never come about at all. Christian hope, on the other hand, conversely draws the future into the present, because the divine future becomes the present in the crucified Christ. Here is where the future arrives." [20]

The keen sense of dependence we have just been describing leads us now to consider what emerges as a third aspect of hopeful prayer: the extraordinary dialectic of acceptance and rebellion. For an overemphasis upon dependence, focusing as it does upon the eventual triumph of God's love and our anticipation of this triumph here and now, inevitably tends to minimize the tragedy in human life as well as God's ultimate responsibility for it. Such tragedy, however, may not be minimized, under penalty of making both prayer and hope an escape. What is at stake here is not at all the theological problem of the relationship between God's goodness and his omnipotence, nor the relation of these to man's capacity for free decision. What we are talking about is simply the ability to survive the total experience of a human life without ceasing either to pray or to hope. To do so the Christian simply must have the capacity to rebel, not against God but before God. He simply has to be able to express his acceptance and awe of the mystery of suffering and death by asking "Why?"—not indeed as a question seeking an answer but as an exclamation. The language which God speaks to man is not primarily words but events, and an event which crushes or destroys must be challenged if one is ultimately to accept it.

This dialectic of rebellion and acceptance is vividly illustrated in the Psalms as well as in the Book of Job. In the former we find countless examples of perplexity, anger and desolation at the course of events, all of which are prayed aloud before the God who acts in these events: "Hear my voice, O God, as I complain" (Ps. 64, 2). Or consider the pain and violent language of

Psalm 58: "O God, break the teeth in their mouths, tear out the fangs of these wild beasts, O Lord! Let them vanish like waste that runs away: let them wither like grass that is trodden underfoot: let them be like the snail that dissolves into slime; like a woman's miscarriage that never sees the sun." Or listen to the alternation of complaint and trust in Psalm 22:

> My God, my God, why have you forsaken me?
> You are far from my plea and the cry of my distress.
> O my God, I call by day and you give no reply;
> I call by night and I find no peace.
>
> Yet you, O God, are holy. . . .
> In you our fathers put their trust;
> They trusted and you set them free.
> When they cried to you, they escaped. . . .
>
> But I am a worm and no man,
> the butt of men, laughingstock of the people.
> All who see me deride me.
> They curl their lips, they toss their heads.
>
> Yes, it was you who took me from the womb,
> entrusted me to my mother's breast. . . .
> Do not leave me alone in my distress;
> come close, there is none else to help.

Many more examples could be cited. "O God, listen to my prayer, do not hide from my pleading, attend to me and reply; with my cares, I cannot rest" (Ps. 55, 2-3). "Repay them, God, for their crimes; in your anger cast down the peoples. You have kept a record of my tears" (Ps. 56, 8-9). "You have burdened me with bitter troubles but you will give me back my life. . . . You will exalt me and console me again" (Ps. 71, 20-21). The point of all these texts is the same: man cannot endure a fully human life without God, for the burden is too great and the mystery too deep. But while it is normal for man to stumble and to resent the cause of his stumbling (and to present this resentment to God), it is also normal for God to support man, to give him courage and confidence and trust, for "he remembered they were only men, a breath that passes never to return" (Ps. 78, 39).

In the Book of Job this dialectic is even clearer. Contrary to the popular stereotype, Job is the most impatient of men. His complaints to God fill whole chapters: "Why is light given to him that is in misery, and life to the bitter in soul, who long for death but it comes not. . . ? Why is light given to a man whose way is hid, whom God has hedged in? . . . I am not at ease nor am I quiet; I have no rest, but trouble comes" (Jb. 3, 20-26). The clearest message from Job's tortured experience is that the goodness of God does not involve good things happening to those who hope in him; nor does the way things go depend upon one's deserts. "Events do not constitute evidence for the goodness of God, since the essence of the believer's belief in divine goodness consists precisely in the fact that the meaning of life does not depend on how it goes." [21] This is clearly the meaning of the questions God asks Job in chapters 38ff: "Where were you when I laid the foundation of the earth? . . . Who determined its measurements —surely you know! . . . Have you entered into the springs of the sea or walked in the recesses of the deep? Will you ever put me in the wrong? Will you condemn me that you may be justified?" This appearance of God at the end of the book makes almost irrelevant the question of whether and how the world of events depends upon him; it is *Job* who depends on God, not indeed for explanations but for life. God's revelation of himself as someone utterly beyond Job's comprehension enables him finally to accept a life which is likewise beyond his comprehension. His own rebellion before God becomes thereby an entry into mystery.

III

"The only thing that counts," writes St. Paul, "is new creation." [22] What we have tried to do in the preceding pages is to indicate two approaches to the personal and the mysterious, that of time and that of hope, which might be of help in approaching fruitfully the contemporary problem of prayer. In reality what we have been talking about is one aspect of the Christian's participation in the creative action of God, namely that conscious aspect by which the personal and the mysterious in God are brought home most vividly to the believer. For creativity takes place in time and the responsibility of hope is the creative act itself. Prayer consequently is very much concerned with decision, since decision-making in a very real sense is the process of determining the creative will of God. The "new creation" spoken of by Paul, while essentially an eschatological hope, is thus in part also a present realization. Participation in such creation involves a constant awareness that the God who is with us will also surprise us. Frequently this surprise comes in the form of new beauty that suddenly releases the hope dimension in life. Hope is then belief that this particular beauty can actually be realized, either in oneself or in others or in this world, and without it no man would ever take a step to bring such beauty into existence.

Yet even when man fails in his search for beauty, this failure can itself be creative by becoming a participation in the cross of Christ, which is as much part of the time process as is the resurrection. In a society where success is the dominant motive, the cross stands as a reminder, not that failure is good, but that it is human, that it can never be ruled out of any truly human life, and that it always contains within itself the possibility of a new beginning. The need we have for God in prayer is thus not that of a problem solver but that of a support. This support of God is gentle and gracious, like his presence to Elijah in "the sound of a gentle whisper," for man must also support himself in his failures by using his initiative and freedom. Such free response to the mystery of life is, by this subtle action of God, harmonized somehow with God's ultimate design to make men like himself. "History is the business of making personalities," writes Herbert Butterfield, "even so to speak by putting them through the mill; its very vicissitudes bring personality to a finer texture." [23] While the Christian's optimism cannot be immature, therefore, it must not cease to be optimism. After all the events which count against such optimism have been accepted, his characteristic attitude toward the present and future will still be one of hope, looking upon temporal reality as the stage upon which God works out his designs. These designs will remain, however, long after man has said whatever there is to say, the greatest mystery of all.

III

Toward a Theology
of the Future

America is unique, it has been said, because it is the first society actually to experience the future. Concretely this experience is one of accelerating change oriented toward what has been called a "technetronic" or "cybernetic" society. At a much faster pace than the rest of the world, cultural, social and economic life in America is being altered today by the power of technology and autonomous control systems. The extraordinary sense of awe which everywhere accompanied viewings of the recent moon flights underscores this sudden awareness that we shall be living in a new type of world sooner than we think. Sober scientists accept as certainties man's power within the next century to eliminate famine and disease, to accumulate knowledge in electronic banks and transmit it directly to the human brain through the nervous system, to stabilize population, even to "engineer" man's genetic development. These predictions are based, it should be noted, not on flights of imagination but upon techniques already known and in operation, by which man commits himself to the future in and through decisions made in the present.

This experience of a future rapidly moving into the present has resulted in America in an especially strong desire for both accurate forecast and responsible control. This double desire has in turn given rise to a series of problems which touch contemporary man as man, and, as a consequence, contemporary Christian theology. What has come to be called "the theology of the future" owes much of its appeal to the fact that it attacks these problems directly, providing not answers so much as a context from Christian revelation for their fuller comprehension. In the pages that follow we shall first briefly outline some of the concrete manifestations of this desire for forecast and control as well as some of the reasons for theology's sudden interest in rethinking the Christian message in function of this contemporary orientation of man and his world. We shall then sketch in broad outline the theology of the future now developing, with this emphasis upon hope as the organizing principle of revelation. Finally we shall indicate some of the practical consequences for Christian life now being drawn from this change in theological perspective.

I

In the summer of 1967 an entire issue of *Daedalus* was devoted to deliberations of the American Academy of Arts and Sciences' Commission on the Year 2000. Among its riches was a preliminary report by Herman Kahn and his associates at the Hudson Institute, published subsequently in expanded form as a book, *The Year 2000*. Kahn attempts first to identify long-range trends in America likely to continue into the next century: the worldwide spread of secular humanism, institutionalization of scientific innovation, and continuous economic growth. He then explores a number of "alternative worlds," as he calls them, "scenarios" of future possibilities, worked out from extrapolations based on different sets of assumptions. What is important for us here is to note that his efforts, and those of many others, to forecast the future inevitably focus at the start upon scientific and technological progress already begun and which can reasonably be expected to continue more or less at the same rate. The structure of society within which such developments will take place, however, and the use to which they will be put, are much more problematic, and depend upon what man decides to do with and in the world he is creating. Precisely because his areas of choice are widening rapidly, man is coming to feel uneasy. The more the consequences of his self-made world become incalculable, the greater is his desire for forecast and the more confused he becomes about ultimate meanings and goals. For of itself secular culture can provide him only with short-range, pragmatic means, while the ends to which they are directed, the "alternative worlds," will depend upon value judgments which he has perhaps carelessly made in the past and feels at a loss to make now.

Many thoughtful observers have noted this anomaly in the present outlook on the future. In the Fall 1962 issue of *Technology and Culture,* Jacques Ellul asks how man is to remain master in a world of means, and answers that as yet there is no answer. An individual can inquire after the values to impose on technology, and can also search out the way to remain a man in the fullest sense within a "technetronic" society. But these efforts of the individual are in themselves pointless to resolve in any way the problem in its totality, since to accomplish that would require that *all* men in a given society adopt the same values and the same behavior. In a pluralistic culture, however, such concern for ultimate meanings, which alone makes hope of humanization possible, is not a unitive but a divisive force. Hence the insistence of Fred Charles Iklé, in the issue of *Daedalus* already mentioned, that predictions for the year 2000 not attempt to *describe* our world but rather to evaluate the *consequences* of alternative courses of action. For any aspect of the future whose consequences do not depend upon our choice here and now is really irrelevant. What man needs, then, is to see the full extent of his burden of freedom and somehow gain the necessary strength to support it.

Nor are there lacking those who deny that such support is likely to be obtained. C. P. Snow has said that "the signs are all pointing the wrong way—objective grounds for hope have gotten less and less and the objective grounds for nonhope have gotten stronger. I have been nearer to despair this year, 1968, than ever in my life." [1] *Homo sapiens,* writes Arthur Koestler in *The Ghost in the Machine,* must have some error or deficiency built into the wiring circuits of his brain. Otherwise how explain his urge to self-destruction and proneness to delusion, or his extraordinary impulse to make war upon his own species in the name of self-made idols? He must be some kind of biological freak, the result of some remarkable mistake in the evolutionary process. On the level of society this same conviction underlies Herbert Marcuse's *One-Dimensional Man.* He sees the United States fast becoming the most irrational of societies in respect to the values of truth and human living. So hedonistic is its culture, so object-oriented and repressive of the individual, that the only cure seems to be some total regenerative effort destroying the whole system. While technology provides man with material well-being, it has also produced in America a "state of anesthesia," which either absorbs or streamlines all "existence-transcending" forces which oppose it. Today the discrepancy between the emancipation of man's freedom which is possible and the repression which is practiced is greater than it ever was before.

What these writers have done, each in his own way, is to touch the nerve center of modern man's anxiety before a future which, in spite of the accuracy of technological prediction, remains unstructured precisely in areas that concern him most personally. "Tomorrow?" asks Teilhard de Chardin. "But who can guarantee us a tomorrow anyway? And without the assurance that this tomorrow exists, can we really go on living, we to whom has been given—perhaps for the first time in the whole history of the universe—the terrible gift of foresight?" [2] What man wants is not greater power to *invent* the future, of which he may already have too much, but greater power to *plan* it, to plan those fulfillments of himself and his society which he has not yet found either in his present or his past. This means looking to the future as a way out from a one-dimensional, utopianless world, an arena where new possibilities can finally be realized, not for technology so much as for human community, where the unfinished character of existence can be redeemed at last. What contemporary man wants most is to actualize "the hope principle" in the depths of his being, that mystique of transcendence rooted in a world of restive change. And what contemporary American man wants is to dream once more the American dream.

What have all these developments, both in America and the world at large, to do with Christian theology? For our answer we must take briefly into account two large areas of current religious concern. The first is the fundamental question of the relation between theology and the world view of a given culture. There are those like sociologist Peter Berger who have warned that efforts to accommodate religious affirmations to psychological reality structures can become an abdication of theological responsibility in favor of "market research." For in a pluralist society, says Berger, religion resembles a commodity obliged to compete on the open market. But such an endeavor to "sell" the Christian faith can result, as it has in the case of the radical theologians, in a complete secularist revolution. The tactical problem of getting one's message across to a recalcitrant clientele has a built-in escalation factor: the clientele is likely to become more, not less, recalcitrant in the pluralizing situation. If reality structures of the man in the street are allowed to become the unquestioned standard of cognitive validity, they will necessarily tend to bring with them all the uncertainty that comes from long confrontation with various reality-defining agencies, none of which has compelled allegiance. The question is, therefore, given the problem of translation, which are the grammars to be used and how? The newly refined tools of biblical and historical scholarship have already become a prominent part of translation procedures, as well as ideas from psychoanalysis, existentialism, sociology and linguistic analysis. But many theologians who use these tools seem to be unaware that modern man's outlook, which the tools themselves represent, is the result not of some intrinsically superior access to truth but of his existence in a pluralist environment which in fact tends to undermine religious certitude. The enthusiasm of the theologians for adaptation should consequently be tempered with extreme caution, since from the sociological and historical point of view the attitudes of our present age are, cognitively speaking, as relative as those of any other.[3]

Now this skepticism toward adaptation, whether on the part of sociologists like Berger or on the part of those who, unlike him, feel that defense is the only proper theological attitude, arises from a misunderstanding which can perhaps be clarified by considering a second large area of current religious concern, namely the problem of God. Everyone is aware that this problem arises today from the fact that in the past the experience of God was to a large extent that of a substitute for powers which man himself lacked. No longer, however, does man need such a God. No longer must he appeal to him for solace or assistance in his helplessness before a world he cannot control. His grasp of the secular sphere is now firm and bold, and demands no recourse to religion to support it. Nevertheless, while *this* role of God is rapidly disappearing in modern culture, it does not follow that this same culture will not be the occasion for a new experience of God coming to birth in harmony with the forces of social and psychological change. Christianity's apparent inability as yet clearly to formulate such an experience in conceptual terms is simply testimony that it has not yet dissociated itself from one cultural pattern nor completely made the transition into the one now developing. "In the past," writes Edward Schillebeeckx, "God was an accepted idea—he was the world mover, the last cause, he upheld the moral and political order of the world, and even maintained social stability. In the modern world God has ceased to be an idea and has become a question which both believers and nonbelievers are never tired of discussing in ordinary conversation, in the newspapers, in books and articles, and on the radio and television. Now that we can no longer feel secure with ideas of God, God himself is the subject of our conversations." [4]

It is not a question, therefore, as Berger suggests, of adaptation by grudging concessions to a recalcitrant clientele in order once again to "sell" Christianity and make it "marketable." Rather there is question of a new understanding of Christian revelation in and through the experience of a new culture. For God can only be known in relation to the particular world in which men live. Any self-revelation on his part which lay outside a given sphere of human experience simply could not be heard.[5] What makes our knowledge of God what it is are the specific cultural factors which make our world what it is. These cultural factors, however, are in turn becoming more and more characterized by a thrust toward the future. Science and technology have given man the possibility of changing the earth and planning the well-being of mankind as a whole. Such goals are in fact totally new in human history and rivet attention not on the world as it has been and is, but on the world that is to come into being. Such changes in man's experience must necessarily also affect his experience of God, for he cannot be oriented toward the future by his whole culture and pulled toward the past by his religion; his concept of God cannot be relevant to his life if it is at odds with his society.

Now the contemporary theology of the future is precisely an attempt to come to grips with and to articulate the relationships between God and man as these are now being experienced in a culture slowly coming to birth. Adaptation of this type is in fact a new questioning of the biblical witness to Christ, one which arises from our peculiar difficulty in speaking about and to God in our contemporary world. The same inquiry was not possible for Christians of a former generation simply because they were living in *their* world, not ours. Nor can the Scriptures satisfy our questioning immediately, since their message was directed to men whose inquiry was very different. "The Gospel does not answer questions that are not asked. . . . Every generation asks the Gospel its own questions from the context of its own life. . . . The answer the Gospel gives us will therefore be new, but at the same time also *evangelical*. This presupposes that we should be ready . . . to change, extend or correct our questioning in the light of Scripture and biblical interpretation given during the Church's whole history." [6] What the theology of the future is ultimately asking, then, is not so much how the Christian today should speak about God (although this is obviously a problem), but how God through Christ now speaks to us, that is to say, how Christian faith is to function and be expressed in our new culture without becoming identified with it. Jesus himself, then, as proclaimed by the faith of the apostles, is the guiding principle of readaptation. Through him the Gospel inspires our questioning, and this questioning itself necessarily interprets the Gospel in confrontation with our future-oriented culture.

II

The theology of the future may be discussed from two points of view. The first centers upon an effort to rethink in terms of hope the totality of Christian revelation, with eschatology as the organizing principle. The second concerns itself with the practical consequences in the Christian life that follow such a change in theological perspective. The names most frequently associated with the first point of view are Jürgen Moltmann [7] and Wolfhart Pannenberg,[8] and with the second, Edward Schillebeeckx,[9] Karl Rahner,[10] Johannes Metz [11] and Harvey Cox.[12] Two others, the German Marxist Ernst Bloch [13] and the French Jesuit Pierre Teilhard de Chardin,[14] elaborated their own systems of thought long before present concern for the future, but their writings continue today to be a source of inspiration both for theory and practical application.

The speculative approach of Moltmann and Pannenberg has to be seen historically as a reaction to the thought of Rudolf Bultmann and others in the same tradition, who see New Testament concern for the future in terms of the existential decision of man to the "now" of revelation. Such a theology tends indeed to individualize and spiritualize eschatology; it interprets revelation primarily as the disclosure of the eternal transcendence breaking into time, and understands the Parousia of Christ as his presence rather than his return. This approach, according to its critics, serves only to imprison man in his own finitude and to falsify the central biblical view of revelation as both promise and future fulfillment. Hence the dialogue which these critics of Bultmann carry on with the Marxist Ernst Bloch, and the use they make of his philosophical categories of "not-yet-being," "frontier," and "the new." These categories serve as antidotes to what they believe to be the deleterious influence upon Bultmann of Martin Heidegger. In Bloch's system hope is the key to an understanding of man, "the hoping animal" with an "infatuation for the possible," whose innate power is to project himself into the future. Bloch acknowledges, moreover, that it was through the Hebrew-Christian Scriptures that man first realized his innate power of courageously living for a new and better world. "Christian theology," writes Pannenberg, "will be indebted to Ernst Bloch's philosophy of hope if it again finds the courage to deal with its central category: the general concept of eschatology. . . . Bloch has taught us to understand anew the overwhelming significance of a future which is still open, and of the hope which anticipates this future, for the life and thought of mankind and for the ontological peculiarity of all reality. He has regained the eschatological method of thinking of the biblical traditions as a theme for philosophical reflection and also for Christian theology." [15]

The theology of the future, then, wishes to construct an ontology and an anthropology (Pannenberg emphasizing the former, Moltmann the latter) which will understand the future as a divine mode of being and hope as the "thermal current" in all articles of the Christian faith. The revelation to Israel which culminated in Jesus is where the promise of this future is to be found. Israel lived as a people in the light of God's promises, first to Abraham, then to his descendants, to Moses and the prophets. In contrast to the Hellenic view of life where "future" was meaningless, the Hebrews lived in continual expectation. This is confirmed by reading the divine name in Exodus 3, 14 as "I will be who I will be," so that God is seen to be the "God before us," whose transcendence is revealed precisely as the force of our future. We know this "God before us" in the unfolding history of his promises. Again, in the resurrection of Jesus, God is seen as the one who has raised and will raise the dead. In this event we see something totally new, which in turn is itself a pledge of Christ's lordship over the whole cosmos, a lordship "not yet" actualized but promised. While the accent of Jesus' message differed from the Jewish eschatological hope insofar as he underscored the present impact of the future, this difference cannot be so exaggerated that the futurity of the Kingdom in his message is minimized. "Jesus indeed spoke of the presence of the Kingdom of God, but always in terms of the presence of God's *coming* Kingdom. Futurity is fundamental for Jesus' message." [16]

Both Moltmann and Pannenberg insist upon this centrality of the resurrection for any Christian experience of the presence of the future. "In remembering this one, unique event, we remember the hope for the future of all world history. . . . The expectation of what is to come on the ground of the resurrection of Christ, must then turn all reality that can be experienced and all real experience into an experience that is provisional and a reality that does not yet contain within it what is held in prospect for it." [17] Though the two men understand the historicity of the resurrection differently (Pannenberg stressing the possibility and necessity of knowing it by modern standards of historical research [18]), the event itself is clearly the guarantee for both that in the fullness of Jesus the fullness of the whole world is to be realized. It thus provides a hermeneutic principle for judging the Christian proclamation of a future promised but not yet realized. "This event which is revealed in the cross and the Easter experiences points back to the promises of God and forward to an *eschaton* in which his divinity is revealed in all. It must then be understood as the eschatological coming to pass of the faithfulness of God, and at the same time as the eschatological authentication of his promise and as the dawning of its fulfillment. . . . Jesus identifies himself in the Easter appearances as the coming one, and his identity in cross and resurrection points the direction for coming events and makes a path for them. . . . What happened to him is understood as the dawn and assured promise of the coming glory of God over all, as the victory of life from God over death." [19]

Yet the centrality of the resurrection must not in any way obscure the reality of the cross in the Christian orientation toward the future. For the real problem of all thinking in terms of hope is the fact of death. Hope in the future can be taken seriously by the Christian only if death is taken seriously. Such hope can thus never be equated with security. It is not an attempt to rob the future of mystery, or to develop a glorified optimism about progress that somehow shuts its eyes to the hard realities of life, especially that suffering must eventually be the lot of every human being. The final outcome of Jesus' earthly life is in this sense a confirmation that by all human standards the life of man is more tragic than triumphant. Only Jesus' resurrection, made accessible to the Christian through faith, brings the conviction that our immediate experience of life is not an ultimate experience. This hoped-for-future of man, both individual and collective, thus has in its favor neither facts nor auspicious tendencies on the part of nature, but only the faithfulness of God who stands by his Word and his promise. Christian hope is thus a hope contrary to what is seen, as Paul says in Romans 8, 24. Because of the resurrection of Christ who was crucified the Christian can, in the face of death, set his hope on the impossible. The person who trusts in the crucified Christ can in fact surrender to life completely, since death and the pain of a continual self-giving in love ultimately has life both as its source and its achievement.[20]

From what has been said thus far, it will readily be seen why the centrality of the resurrection in the theology of the future inevitably leads it to focus upon the doctrine of God. For the only future to which Christian eschatology can be oriented is what Karl Rahner has called "the absolute future" and Pannenberg, "the ultimate future." All intermediate futures are more or less in the hands of men and must inevitably become pasts, since their achievements will always be partial, and flawed by the ambiguities of suffering and death. But to think in these terms is to raise the question of the future as a divine mode of being. "The future as a mode of being of God has still not been considered in theology, in spite of the close correlation of God and of the coming reign of God in the eschatological message of Jesus. . . . As the power of the future, the God of the Bible has always been and is still beyond any statements made about him, and he has already surpassed every conception of God. . . . The power of the future—and only it—can be an object of hope and trust; for the future has power over that which is temporally present and releases the forces that overcome it." [21]

By thus conceiving God primarily as the power of the future, Pannenberg can speak of the present as an effect of the future in contrast to the conventional assumption that past and present cause the future. This priority of the ultimate future demands, he says, a reversal in our ontological conceptions. "In every event the infinite future separates itself from the finite events which until then had been hidden in this future but are now released into existence. The future lets go of itself to bring into being our present. . . . In every present we confront the infinite future, and in welcoming the particular finite events which spring from that future, we anticipate the coming of God." [22] This concept of the futurity of God, however, does not mean that God is only in the future and not in the past and present as well. For as power of the future he dominates the remotest past. Nor does such a concept exclude that of eternity: "The God of the coming Kingdom must be called eternal because he is not only the future of our present but has been also the future of every past age. . . . He was the future even of that 'nothing' which preceded creation." Such futurity does not therefore imply any development of God, for "what turns out to be true in the future will then be evident as having been true all along." This applies especially to truth about God. "God was present in every past moment as the one who is in his futurity. He was in the past the same one whom he will manifest himself to be in the future." [23]

What Pannenberg is insisting upon, then, is the ontological priority of the future as this becomes evident in the idea of God as the one who is coming. Such rethinking of the doctrine of God in the context of the eschatological message of Jesus constitutes an essential first step in making hope the "thermal current" in all articles of the Christian faith. For to associate the transcendence of God with the absolute future of man is, in a culture oriented toward the future, to enable divine transcendence to have a new significance for the believer. God the wholly Other now becomes God the wholly New. In Jesus Christ this God gives to the world the possibility and responsibility of transcending its past and creating what has never been before. This "new" is not a mere renewal; it can even be, as Paul says in 1 Corinthians 2, 7, the entrance of the totally unexpected, a future determined by the absolute freedom of God. Although faith still has priority in the Christian life, hope would now have the primacy, to use Moltmann's phrasing. Without faith's knowledge of Christ human hope would indeed become a mere utopia hanging in the air; but without hope faith becomes fragmented and ultimately dies. It is hope that enables faith to move toward the future and to draw the believer into love; and therefore it will also be hope which mobilizes faith's thinking and reflection upon human nature, history and society. "Faith hopes in order to know what it believes," says Moltmann, and this is why he can call for Christian theology to follow a new basic principle: *spes quaerens intellectum—spero ut intellegam*.[24] "If one succeeds in conceiving God and the future together," he writes, "then one can see the future in the past, the *eschaton* as initial purpose, transformation in expiation, the Kingdom of God in the resurrection of Christ, and the promised land in the Gospel. An eschatological ontology and anthropology will then be able to consider transient matter together with its future, reconciling them with mortal human existence seen together with its glorification. This will be possible because in both (and here we have the most important consideration) the power of the divine future can be made manifest in nothingness itself." [25]

III

The changes in theological perspective we have just outlined have opened up a number of problem areas in concrete Christian living, and to these the nascent theology of the future has also been addressing itself. First, however, it has had to defend its right to do so. For it can be readily seen how constant orientation toward the future, in reaction to existentialist theology, could be understood only as an emphasis elaborated at the expense of the present. By concentrating on those past events in salvation history in which God's promises for the future are most clearly manifest, such an emphasis, it is argued, tends to absorb the present either into its past foundation or its future development. Both Moltmann and Pannenberg are sensitive to this kind of criticism and have accordingly taken pains to indicate the importance they attach to the present. Moltmann writes that "the new is never totally new," and "the place where the future of man and of the world is decided is the present, which is the frontline of the future." [26] His statements that hope's promises always stand in "contradiction to present reality" must not therefore be understood literally.[27] Pannenberg, on the other hand, points to his conviction that God as ultimate future gives a transcendent worth to every present moment. "The future comes to be relevant through the fact that it 'comes into' the present. . . . The confession of the incarnation of God in Jesus Christ affirms, in this sense, that in him the future of God has become present among us, and not only a transitory present . . . but an enduring present—through the spirit of Jesus—because it is a present that has an unbounded future." [28]

Nevertheless, it is not Moltmann and Pannenberg who have developed the full practical implications of these statements, but rather theologians like Johannes Metz and Edward Schillebeeckx, the former through his "political theology," the latter through his description of the Church's function of "critical negativity." Both emphasize that the Christian's eschatological hope, far from disengaging him from the present, forces him to view it as the time for decision; not passive dreams for the future but practical initiatives in the present are called for. For the miseries of the world around us become intolerable in the light of the new creation promised by Christ. To hope, then, is not simply to trust in God but to commit oneself to changing a society always open in its possibilities. It is this joining of hope to realizable possibility which makes it practical, and gives rise to that relationship which exists between that critical character of Christian hope and the contemporary instinct for planning. To plan the future is consciously to execute the transition from the possible to the real. The finite futures which man thereby realizes, however, must always be recognized as finite; they can never be seen as exhausting the possibilities of human development. Human planning can foster man's growth in freedom but only in the absolute future can this freedom be fully actualized through the powerful intervention of God. Consequently there must remain a dialectical tension between what is planned by man and what is unforeseen by him, what is anticipated and what comes through the unexpected intervention of God. For the dynamics of "grace" touch the actions of all men, Christian and non-Christian alike, and it is this conviction which gives to Christian hope its desire to cooperate with God in bringing to pass in the present not simply the possible but the new.[29]

For Johannes Metz all this can be summarized by the term "political theology." He sees, first of all, an intrinsic relationship between the changing of the world under the free hand of man, and the eschatological horizon of promise. On this horizon the world appears not as a finished reality but as one in process toward a greater future through man's free decision. The Christian doctrine of creation, moreover, as well as the clear acceptance of the transcendence of God, is what historically deprived the world of its divine character in the eyes of men and provided thereby a basis for its new evaluation and use. Once man saw the world as finite, he realized that he had the power, as co-worker with God, to control nature and set it to his own purposes. In

Christ God accepts this world of man, and through the Incarnation asserts the full reality both of himself and of the world, at the same time making manifest their eventual convergence. Christian hope for the future thus cannot be fulfilled if the world and its future are passed over; such hope clings to a single promised future which includes the future of the world. Hence the responsibility of hope can best be expressed in the concept of "creative eschatology," by which Metz means that the contents of the promise founded on Jesus—freedom, peace, justice, reconciliation—require the assumption of social responsibility. Nor does this mean to identify the Christian promise with any historical condition of society; on the contrary, such identification would involve a surrender of that "eschatological reservation" by reason of which every historically attained status of society appears provisional. Rather what is important is to see that the Christian ought to approach the world's future not by contemplating it but by bringing it about through historical demands that are "political" in a truly theological sense.[30]

"I understand political theology," writes Metz, "to be a critical correction of present-day theology inasmuch as this theology shows an extreme privitizing tendency (a tendency, that is, to center upon the private person rather than 'public,' 'political' society). At the same time I understand this political theology to be a positive attempt to formulate the eschatological message under the conditions of our present society." [31] In itself, therefore, such a theology is less a question of social involvement than one of theological epistemology: the Christian message does not attribute to the socio-political reality some shadowy existence, but regards it as an area with which Christian salvation is intrinsically concerned. Here Metz is reacting, like Moltmann and Pannenberg, against what he calls a theology of transcendental, existential, personalist orientation, whose most prominent categories are of the intimate, the private, the apolitical sphere. Charity is here regarded as the virtue of the I-Thou relation extending to the field of interpersonal encounter, or at best to charity on the scale of the neighborhood. Whereas Christian love must also mobilize itself socially as an unconditional determination toward justice and freedom, and this must be accomplished through the

Church as an institution of criticism in society, radically oriented to the future rather than to the maintenance of the *status quo*.[32]

At this point Metz's approach to the question touches that of Edward Schillebeeckx. The latter explains his concept of "critical negativity" as a positive power exercising constant pressure to bring about what is most desirable for man in the future, not by explicit formulation but by negative knowledge. "In the long run, situations which are unworthy of man give rise to explicit protest, not in the name of a concept of what . . . is already positively defined, but in the name of human values still being sought and revealed in a negative manner in the contrast-experience of situations unworthy of man. The Christian has as little positive idea as the non-Christian of what is worthy of man, either ultimately or here and now. He too has to seek fumblingly and consider various alternatives, keeping in the back of his mind, as he searches, human values already realized in history." [33] The difference, however, for the Christian is that his eschatological faith in the God of the promise tells him that even though he cannot form the content of the promise in a positive way, God has nonetheless bound himself to the realization of this promise in Christ. What is humanly possible becomes really possible in Jesus.

The Christian's hope thus makes him critical of every attempt to realize a perfect future for the whole of mankind purely on the basis of technological planning. For this would be to attribute solely to the power of man the future he is in process of achieving, whereas in fact the future promised to him by God must be received as a gift. Nor is such reception a purely passive act, since the future so received must thereafter be "made" by man himself. Precisely because those who make history are sinful men, the realization of a better future cannot come simply from planning but must also come from redemption. Eschatological hope says that everything really worthy of man is possible through the resources of man himself, but this means the resources of *redeemed* man. For it is the sinfulness of man which is continually forcing the question whether what is worthy of man is ultimately possible at all. The Christian answer is that it *is* possible, but only if man is open to a transcendence of himself and all his limitations. The critical function of the Church is thus directed at everything which would diminish man's being, against every skepticism of man's potential, against every attempt to consider him exclusively as either matter or means for building a completely rationalized technological future. "The distinctively Christian contribution is to be found," concludes Schillebeeckx, "on the one hand, in a commitment to the building up of the world by a concern for man which is radical for the sake of eschatological faith and implemented by all available scientific and technical means, and on the other hand, in a criticism which is based on and inwardly flows from this same Christian hope, a criticism that is directed toward every positive design of man which is presented as the last word or which in any way diminishes man's being." [34]

We may end this discussion of the practical consequences of eschatology in Christian life with the theory advanced by Pierre Teilhard de Chardin to explain man's relationship to God in the creation of the future. Teilhard saw the world which man achieves as a "preliminary sketch" or "rough draft" of the final outcome of the evolutionary process. Man plans and works for the new earth in accordance with his own aspirations and desires, but his achievement must be refinished and brought to completion by God, just as the work of art begun by the apprentice is completed by the master artist. Thus in the incipient interiority of plants Teilhard saw a "rough sketch" of consciousness, and in the primates he saw a "first draft" of the human person. The structure of human personality at present is therefore only a "faint sketch" of that collectivity of consciousness to emerge at the final state of the universe. Scientific cooperation, racial integration, international harmony, these likewise represent an "outline" only of that total sense of humanity to become manifest in the future. Transformation, then, is in Teilhard's thought an analogous concept used to describe the part which God plays at every stage of man's making of man; the divine hand refinishing the preliminary sketch made by the human hand, and at the Parousia transforming the whole of history. Christian hope thus becomes the creative dynamism enabling man to advance into a future that often terrifies him by its newness and disheartens him by its uncertainty. Because the promised goal of history is the *pleroma* of Christ, the Christian should have an immense and totally human hope, one which constitutes an invitation for Christ to return.[35] Harvey Cox has noted that Teilhard's approach here transcends ordinary teleological approaches by placing in human hands the key to the next stage of the cosmic process. What next happens really *is* up to man. In such a perspective teleology ripens indeed into prophecy, which is the characteristically Hebrew mode of perceiving the future as the open field of human hope and responsibility.[36]

IV

The broad outlines of the theology of the future which we have sketched here would seem to justify two concluding remarks. The first is that there is danger in the type of optic we have been discussing only through exclusivity. If one can say in a perfectly correct sense that hope is an unfolding of faith, then one must also say that such unfolding is at the same time an orientation of faith toward the future. What one cannot say is that this dimension of the future is the whole of faith. For faith is oriented also toward the past whence it takes its origin, and toward the present where it actually exists. This is why faith has to be the comprehensive principle in theology. While hope obviously comes from faith, faith cannot be explained exclusively in terms of hope. The creed and its contents are more than their future dimension. The author of Hebrews 11, 1 says that faith is hope's foundation, its origin and the measure of its truth. Faith must therefore have not only the priority but also the primacy. Contrary to Moltmann's view, *credo ut intelligam* remains more fundamental than *spero ut intelligam*. The latter enables us to catch the inner unity of God's promises given through the Old and New Testaments. But the life of Jesus is more than an event of promise; it means that grace, justification and salvation are given to man in the present. Only insofar as man *actually* possesses these, can he have hope in God's future promise. In both Moltmann and Pannenberg we find a tendency to limit this existential aspect of soteriology, whereas in fact there is no reason at all for them to do so. The theology of the future they elaborate provides us with a key for reordering all the various elements in revelation, but in doing so it need not exclude or minimize any of the data. The "not yet" cannot do without the "already." [37]

A second conclusion concerns the relationship between this new theological perspective and human freedom. We noted earlier in this chapter man's power today to change himself to a degree previously undreamed of, indeed, to make an experiment of himself. He has in a true sense entered the era of self-creation. As Teilhard saw so clearly, biological evolution has gradually developed into a cultural evolution in which man makes all the decisive choices and does all the systematic planning. Karl Rahner has observed that this development is in no way inimical to Christianity but is in radical harmony with it, since man is now becoming what Christianity has always taught him to be: a free being under his own responsible control. Christianity insists, however, that this human planning, this active self-fulfillment through the manipulation of reality, is embraced by an event not subject to our purposes and beyond all planning. When man pushes forward into the future, he not only sees his own practical achievements, but also experiences what is not his achievement, what is purely given. This mystery of absolute giving the Christian calls God, the mystery of love endlessly giving itself. The Christian finds this mystery in Christ and he confesses it in hope.[38] And it is precisely this eschatological hope which can bring to modern man a sense of security in the God who is to come.

The source of this confidence, it should be noted, is God's living *presence* to man as he creates his own future. There is no question here of appealing to God as a solver of problems or as a refuge from the harshness of life. For what man is afraid of is not his inability to control his world as he moves into the future, but his inability to control himself. What he needs, then, is a reaffirmation, within the context of the future, of the personal relationship between God and himself. "The future of humanity," said the Second Vatican Council, "lies in the hands of those who are strong enough to provide coming generations with reasons for living and hoping." [39] These reasons somehow must assuage man's sense of loneliness in the cosmos, for ultimately it is loneliness which will make his freedom a burden too heavy to bear. "Man, overburdened in his freedom and left alone even by his fellow-men to make free decisions, need not ultimately feel lonely —as St. John observes in a masterly statement in his Gospel, given as a pure interpretation of Jesus' life (John 8:61). 'I am not alone; the Father is always with me.' " [40] Within this sphere of trust, then, and of the constant dialogue between God and man, the impossible can actually be undertaken. Indeed, it is only by encouraging the undertaking of the impossible that Christianity can continue to exercise its mission in the modern world. In this way, "a new impulse becomes possible and is now beginning to take shape in human consciousness. Born of the psychic combination of two kinds of faith—in the transcendent action of a personal God and the innate perfectibility of a world in progress—it is an impulse (or better, a spirit of love) that is truly evolutionary. We can indeed say of it that it is the only kind of spiritual energy capable of causing the formidable human machine, in which, from what we can see, all the future and all the hopes of evolution must henceforth be concentrated, to function at full power, without danger from egotism or from mechanization, and to the full extent of its potentialities." [41]

PART TWO
Soundings for Now

IV

Theology and
Liberal Education

The identity crisis presently experienced by Catholic colleges and universities in the United States is not likely to be resolved in the near future. One key element, however, in this vastly complex problem is certainly the role of theology on the graduate and undergraduate levels. For it is becoming clear that it is precisely in the teaching of theology, more than anywhere else in the academic curriculum, that the illusive identity of the Catholic institution is tending to manifest itself. It may even be true to say that the role of the Catholic college and university in American society has been changing because the role of theology has been changing, and that whether one is optimistic or pessimistic about the future of the institution will ultimately depend upon whether one is optimistic or pessimistic about the future of theology. The focus of the present chapter is the undergraduate college, since it is at this level that the problem is felt most acutely today. We shall briefly discuss three aspects of theology's changing role in the Catholic college: its relationship to liberal education, the content of its curriculum and, perhaps most important, the relation of this curriculum to religious commitment. To put these remarks in context, however, it may be helpful at the start to say a word about the variety of influences now affecting the work of theologians themselves.

Much has been written, especially since the Council, of the sudden confrontation of Catholic theology with all the forces presently transforming modern culture. Theologians have become more sensitive than formerly to developments in technology, to the findings of the social and empirical sciences, and especially to non-Catholic and even non-Christian religious thought. The net result of this confrontation has been a change of style among Catholic theologians. An emphasis on inquiry has replaced an emphasis upon indoctrination; closed confessionalism has rapidly given way to an open ecumenism and genuine concern for the secular; and instead of self-assurance, there is now an acknowledgment that the Church too must search for truth, that this is not the private possession of the few but the common discovery of all. Catholic theology today is consequently much more grounded on experience and on a concern for the human and the personal. A privileged position has been given to the problems and needs of contemporary man. An acute historical consciousness, moreover, nurtured initially by the revolution in biblical scholarship, has revealed the relativity of much of what was formally felt to be absolute. The result has been a rethinking, within an ecumenical context, of traditional doctrinal formulations and systematic theology in general. Participants in such rethinking share a common critical attitude toward their own traditions and are most anxious to understand the riches in the heritage of other churches.[1]

Now this general reorientation of theologians toward their material—biblical, historical, systematic—has resulted in a change of mode in both doing and teaching theology. For the only honest way to teach theology as a discipline undergoing change is to bring the student into the community of inquiry. No longer can a "package" be passed on in lectures, because theologians no longer feel that they have such a package. "Covering the field" has therefore become less important than making connections between tradition and contemporary religious issues. Students themselves want to discover and probe these issues through questions growing out of their own lives. What this has meant is that diverse traditions are now operative within a single Catholic tradition, all of them legitimate interpretations of the Christian faith. Theology is in fact becoming the concern of larger and larger numbers of people, many with little formal theological background, yet who from the vantage point of their own lived experience or their own particular academic discipline now ask questions never raised among theologians of a former age. All this means that the problem areas we are about to discuss need serious rethinking, for they are the result of the impact of all these changes upon theology in the American Catholic college.

I

Following the common opinion of educators, we shall understand "liberal education" to mean the process of transmitting a spiritual heritage from one generation to another through initiation into a culture, that is, into a set of values and ideals—religious, philosophic, artistic, scientific—which are seen as worthy of esteem and hence accepted and lived by a community. In this sense liberal education, though it will include an appreciation of all that humanity has produced, is necessarily different in different cultures (as well as changing in changing cultures), for such education is not merely a means of perfecting the individual student, but also the means whereby a given community perpetuates its way of life. In this broad sense, too, liberal education will be carried on by various agencies, family, school, work, social environments. There are, however, degrees of initiation into a culture, and this brings us to the sphere proper to the college in American life. Its specific part in the educational process is to develop human personality at a mature level in and through the acquisition of knowledge and truth. Granted that the making of human personality includes a broader group of objectives than intellectual growth, still this particular objective is fundamental to all others at a mature level and is that proper to the American college. For it is such growth that enlarges the student's capacity for conscious living, extends the reach and range of his relationships and enables him to take possession of the world about him. He is thus prepared to play a more useful and significant role in the social world of his generation, and consequently to contribute a greater share to the achievement of his community.[2]

An important qualification, however, must be added. Through the acquisition of knowledge and truth the American college as such does not aim at producing a specialist but a well-rounded human being. Its objective is less the acquisition of a given discipline for itself than a grasp of its meaning for one's life as a man. This search for meaning is in fact coming to the center of the American scene, chiefly in reaction to a recent tendency to focus the entire educational process on its vocational end-result. Such a focus is now seen as inadequate in preparing a person to grapple with the novelty of our contemporary technological era, which continually poses the question of finality. "The instantaneous electronic intermeshing of mankind," writes Zbigniew Brzezinski, "will make for an intense confrontation straining social and international peace. In the past differences were livable because of the time and distance that separated them. Today these differences are actually widening, while techtronics are eliminating the two insulants of time and distance. The resulting trauma could create almost entirely different perspectives on life, with insecurity, envy and hostility becoming the dominant emotions for increasingly large numbers of people." [3] The educated man in America tomorrow must consequently be capable not only of providing specialized answers but also of asking larger questions dealing with the meaning for man of the extraordinary changes now taking place in American culture.

This makes it essential for a much greater emphasis to be placed upon human values at every point in the educational process, lest personal existence in American life become increasingly depersonalized. Indeed, on the college level the deepest desire of the student is for his own self-fulfillment, to find himself completely in all his natural powers and capacities, especially through interpersonal relationships. This making of himself, intellectually, morally, socially, has always appeared to man as his greatest achievement, and it is perhaps the major preoccupation of American youth during their undergraduate years. What they seek foremost is some ultimate frame of reference for the countless intellectual and emotional stimuli involved in the maturing process called college, some subjective integration of all those vital forces which the development of their natural powers has suddenly released within them. But all these efforts are radically a matter of free decisions for values in every phase of their personal existence. And it is for this reason that the study of religious belief and religious experience cannot be ignored in their education. For the whole thrust of such belief is to provide and support convictions regarding what is ultimately good and valuable in life, convictions which are in turn able to judge and criticize those larger questions of human conduct and development now being forced upon American society.

In *The Image,* a book he wrote over a decade ago, Kenneth Boulding advanced the theory that a man's free decisions depend upon his subjective knowledge structure or the "image" he has formed of the world. This image is modified by successive messages, presented by experience and mediated through a value system that is itself part of the image. The meaning of the message is the change it produces in the image. This may be a simple addition, a clarification, even sometimes a revolutionary change, as when the message hits some sort of nucleus or supporting structure in the image and the whole thing changes in a quite radical way. This analogy is helpful in understanding what the study of religious influence in human life can do within an academic curriculum. It challenges the undergraduate to reassess his image of the world, his value system. The pluralistic, secular society into which he is entering is by definition, as George Lindbeck has pointed out, one which is guided by short-range, pragmatic considerations on the one hand, and whim and emotion on the other. Thus the student cannot avoid continual exposure at close range to a variety of legitimation systems which undermine each other's credibility and authority. He will tend as a consequence, unless something in his education intervenes, to end up with a haphazard collection of beliefs and values lacking depth and integrative power. For the secular city cannot, as secular, decide about ultimate values and goals. "It provides no clues to the nature of true manhood and womanhood, nor can it fill the daily round with a sense of ultimate purpose and meaning. In short, it does not legitimate the human enterprise. Where there is no vision the people perish; and as secularism is the absence of visions, it teeters on the knife-edge between chaos and tyranny." [4]

An abiding vision of human life and work is, therefore, the aim of any academic study of religion. Otherwise the student will have no rational basis for filtering the short-range values in American culture or for interpreting the often disconcerting events of his own daily life. Religious principles by their very nature foster the development of a thoroughly internal legitimation system which is both comprehensive and humane. They tend to prevent the multiplication of other-directed, market-oriented personalities, guided in their lives by purely personal preference or by the opinions advanced by neighbors, advertising or the latest psychological theory.[5] This facing up to the role of religious values in human life is not limited, it should be noted, to courses in the Christian or non-Christian religions. Such values may in fact be encountered very forcefully in the philosophy class, or through history, literature, psychology or sociology. But when this takes place, it is invariably due to the insight and concern of the individual teacher, who determines in certain circumstances to underline the religious significance of his material. It is not due primarily to the subject matter itself. Only the study of man's religious experience in its various forms is capable in its own right of forcing the student to come to terms with ultimate religious questions. Any underemphasis of such study for reasons of expediency, therefore, or its complete absence in some obligatory form from the college curriculum, must necessarily result in an incomplete product, a student whose growth has been stunted in what is most significant to his own development as a man.

From what has been said thus far, it will be clear that I am advocating some minimum requirement in the area of religious studies for all undergraduates, whether these be Catholic, Protestant or non-Christian. The concrete specification of such a requirement will vary from college to college. In general, however, it should be equal to the minimum requirement in effect for other areas, such as literature, history, or foreign languages. For in some way the goals we have indicated for religious studies must be built into the curriculum; they cannot be attained indirectly or by chance, any more than a student can learn history indirectly or by chance as a by-product of mathematics. If liberal education has any true meaning on the college level, all students must be compelled to examine to some extent the intellectual basis of their convictions about religion and its role in their lives. What this extent might be I shall indicate in a moment. Within this context, moreover, it should be clear that in a Catholic college, Christian and Catholic students should have a special and ample opportunity to examine the intellectual basis of their Christian and Catholic belief. That such an opportunity should remain such and in no way become mandatory will be the burden of much of what follows.

II

The general relationship we have just outlined between religious studies and the goals of the American college, leads us naturally now into a consideration of curriculum content. At the start it might be well to define two terms which will appear frequently in our discussion: religion and theology. Religion as an academic discipline will be understood as the study of ultimate religious values phenomenologically, as these have appeared and continue to appear in human life and history. Theology, on the other hand, is the study of ultimate religious values insofar as these have been embodied in a given tradition, whether Christian or non-Christian, and involve a commitment of faith on the part of the one theologizing. Now I think it can be safely said that one of the first questions Catholic students have in their minds as they begin college today is not the relevance of the Christian tradition for human life but the relevance of any religion at all. It is this relevance which must be seen before Christianity can make any sense for them. Hence their introduction to this fundamental problem should not be a course in one or other aspect of the Christian tradition, but a course centered upon the whole phenomenon of religious experience in human life and history. What this course is called makes little difference, but it should be obligatory. It should likewise be clear to the student that its purpose is to make him aware as an educated man of the role played by religious experience in human history, as well as the meaning which such a phenomenon has today when seen from the perspective and vantage point of contemporary culture. The optic of such a course could in fact be theological, conceived as a necessary introduction to the study of the Christian tradition.[6] But it might also be developed from the viewpoint of the historian of religion, or the sociologist of religion or even the philosopher of religion.

The remainder of the college curriculum should, I would suggest, be made up of the widest possible choice of electives dealing with the most diverse problems in the areas both of theology and religion. In a Catholic college these electives should naturally specialize in all aspects of the Catholic tradition—the Church, sacraments, Christology, etc. No one course should be specified as obligatory, though there should be an obligation to choose one or other elective course in addition to the introductory course described earlier. The aim here is to allow the Catholic student freedom either to explore more deeply his own tradition, or to study the traditions of other Christian churches, or to move into a wider acquaintance with the non-Christian religions. For the Catholic cannot have a truly free commitment to his own religious values, cannot appreciate his own Church's teaching on the ultimate meaning of man, unless he has the opportunity to grasp the significance of these values in relation to, and as seen in, the convictions held by other religious traditions. The Catholic college must provide this, and in the light of its present position in higher education, it must do so more adequately than was necessary in a former generation.

It might well be asked at this point what is distinctively Catholic about such a curriculum. Could it not be present in any American college? How is a college's identity as Catholic seen in such a program? The answer is to be found first of all in the program itself. Such interest in non-Catholic religious thought does not mean that a Catholic college is any less dedicated to Catholicism. On the contrary, it indicates greater dedication. For since the Second Vatican Council the Catholic Church has been oriented outward rather than inward. Catholicism has lost the defensiveness of an earlier epoch in the American experience. To be "Catholic" today means to be open. At present mankind is experiencing a convergence of world religions, and it is precisely through commitment to one's own tradition as it is developing today that such convergence is effected and the advance made. Everyone involved in the ecumenical movement acknowledges this. The Catholic college, however, must reflect its own tradition as this exists today. It cannot afford to be more rigid or exclusive in its religious thinking than the Church herself. The variety of its theology curriculum should therefore reflect the variety of its Church's intense contemporary interest in the religious experience of all men.

Secondly, such a program is distinctively Catholic in the availability to all students, Catholic as well as non-Catholic, of a large number of electives covering all aspects of the Catholic tradition, biblical, historical and systematic. Students at a Catholic college expect to find a sophisticated treatment of the Catholic faith by competent theologians who believe that what they are doing is both important in itself and worthwhile for a student's development. This may indeed be the principal reason for their coming to a Catholic school in the first place. It is not necessary, however, that they be obliged to take any one of these courses or that the courses themselves be given in any special order. To believe otherwise is to believe that Catholic theology is still the organic unity, the "package," which it was even up to a decade ago, whereas in fact there has been a fragmentation in theological thinking which should naturally reflect itself in a certain fragmentation of the theology curriculum. The Catholic Church is not yet in full possession of her new self experienced at the Council, and theologians necessarily manifest this in their approach to data and their willingness to see in a new light the sources of Christian revelation. They now think less in terms of synthesis than in terms of hypothesis, less about the possession of truth than about its quest.

Moreover, since Catholic theology is itself no longer an integrated whole, it cannot be argued that a study of all its aspects is necessary to integrate the curriculum of the Catholic college. This question of curriculum integration in any case is hardly one of serious consequence, since the key question today surely is not whether a student is able to see various disciplines as a whole but whether he can see life as a whole. In his *Idea of a University,* Newman never treats explicitly this subjective integration of personal experience in terms of the meaning of man and an ultimate frame of reference of his activity on earth. The "view" he insisted upon so strongly was rather an objective ordering and harmony of the sciences themselves, a task he vaguely attributed to "that Architectonic Science or Philosophy, whatever it be." However necessary such objective integration may be in the total educational aim, it is certainly not of initial or even prime importance in the American college. Indeed, Newman himself presupposed some subjective integration in terms of human life before such an objective integration was possible. Nor did he ever consider the *Idea* a compendium of educational teaching, but a treatment of a portion only of those questions which enter into the general subject of university education.[7]

Finally, it should be noted that one of the functions of the Catholic college today is to explore the Christian significance of man's total religious experience. Our whole educational process in the West has grossly overemphasized our own tradition. Formerly this attitude found its justification in the fact that we were preparing students to take their place in a culture where little or no occasion would ever present itself to experience, much less to assimilate, non-Western cultures. Today, however, all this has changed and we are rapidly moving toward a single world culture where every man is expected to be a global man, aware of both the needs and experiences of all peoples everywhere. In future decades the total human tradition will therefore be much richer than that of any single tradition, and no man will be considered educated who is not at home in the new culture's total ambit. This means that Christianity too must cease to be the tribal religion it has tended to be until now. Its theology, and first of all its theologians, must be concerned to fit the Christian message of salvation into this larger whole and actually to give it that universal character which it has always claimed to possess. Catholicism today involves an openness to truth wherever it is found; it does not consider itself to be the exclusive possessor of revelation, but is seriously attentive to all the religions of the world. The American college is already rapidly drawing non-Western cultures into its curriculum through the study of their languages, history and religion. The Catholic college must therefore do the same, but its distinctive contribution could well be through its theology. For what Catholic students want is a Christianity through which they can identify with the whole of mankind. They will be drawn to study

Sacred Scripture and the Christian tradition only if they see these not as constricting their global consciousness but as expanding it. Such an aim is indeed a Catholic aim and can be pursued with both flexibility and imagination in the type of curriculum we have outlined.

III

Thus far in our discussion I have tried to show that the purpose of a theology curriculum should be to assist all college students to examine the intellectual basis of their convictions about religion, and to assist Christian and Catholic students to examine the intellectual basis of their Christian and Catholic belief. I have said that, with the exception of some general introduction to the whole problem of religious experience, no single course, either in theology or religion, should be obligatory, though the total requirement may be more than a single introductory course. The reasons advanced until now, however, have not yet come to grips with what is perhaps the most delicate question in the whole contemporary effort to rethink theology's changing role, namely the relationship of curriculum to the religious commitment of the individual student. The problem here is that theology is unlike any other intellectual discipline in that a faith response to God revealing is built into whatever material is being investigated. Now what is not generally recognized in Catholic colleges is that to oblige any college student to study his own faith response, unless he himself freely chooses to do so, is precisely to endanger his personal religious commitment or seriously to hamper its mature development.

It will be helpful at this point clearly to distinguish the two types of commitment just mentioned, namely that present in subject matter and that present in persons. We have seen earlier that, in regard to subject matter, courses in religion focus upon the faith experiences of men not insofar as these are true but insofar as they are phenomena which can be experimentally verified and analyzed. The methodology and purpose of such analysis will depend upon whether one is in the area of sociology of religion, history of religions, or philosophy of religion. But the object of the study in any given instance is not what is believed and adhered to in faith but what can be *observed*. The subject matter of a theology course, however, is precisely what is believed by the one theologizing. Assent to the truth of a given doctrine is therefore built into the material which is being analyzed. Thus, in the area of religion, the Catholic Church could be studied from many points of view, but always as an institution. To study the same Church as the Body of Christ, however, can only be done by accepting as true the religious tradition which testifies to such an affirmation. Hence the classical definition of theology as *fides quaerens intellectum,* which refers not only to the faith of the person theologizing but to the faith content of the subject matter itself.

The faith commitment of the persons, on the other hand, is something very different. A Catholic may teach to Catholics a course in the theology of Luther in which the faith commitment of Luther becomes an object of study. The faith commitment of teacher and students would not be in question here, except accidentally insofar as the study of the one commitment forces a reexamination of the other. Likewise a Protestant could teach a course in the thought of the Council of Trent, of which the faith commitment and implications of the Tridentine decrees would constitute an essential part. Both Catholic and Protestant, provided they had the requisite knowledge, could in turn teach a course in the history of religions to either Catholics or Protestants without the faith commitment of either becoming involved in the study. Moreover, since both religion and theology are intellectual disciplines, their major preoccupation will always be with truth. Of themselves they cannot make students good men or even mature men, for the test of maturity is not what a man knows but how much of what he knows enters as a matter of course into all his value judgments. Thus a Catholic student's personal faith commitment might be deeply and positively affected by a course in religion where faith commitment was never in question at all. Yet the same student, if forced to reflect upon his personal commitment insofar as it was embodied in a course in Catholic theology, could well find such study, for quite extrinsic reasons, an obstacle to faith rather than an enrichment.

Now it is these extrinsic reasons which have to be particularly taken into account today. By and large young Catholics arrive in college with a background of four years in a Catholic secondary school, where they were obliged to take theology courses whose presentation of the faith continually challenged their intellectual and moral commitment as Christians. It is understandable, therefore, that in college they should want freedom to choose for themselves the areas of faith they wish to be deepened, and freedom also to broaden the base of their Catholic religious experience by studying that of other traditions. Such students may now resent what in retrospect they see as an overemphasis upon indoctrination in their earlier years. Although deeply interested in ultimate religious values, they may wish to get a safe psychological distance from these values as they have been embodied in Catholic teaching. They may explicitly desire, in other words, to be in control of their own faith commitment, to escape from its imposition either by parents or teachers or Church authority. The tensions which many of them experience today in regard to this authority make any further obligatory study of Catholic belief very unwise. It would bring them no profit educationally, and religiously it could do them irreparable harm. Obviously the Catholic college is concerned with the growth of the student's faith commitment. But it also makes its own the words of the Second Vatican Council: "It is one of the major tenets of Catholic doctrine that man's response to God in faith must be free," for "only in freedom can man direct himself toward goodness." [8]

Before we conclude, we must add one corollary to our argument, and in so doing distinguish a third type of religious commitment, namely that of the Catholic college as institution. We have already touched upon this earlier in emphasizing that a college as Catholic should reflect the openness of the Church herself in the present age, while at the same time giving a preferential treatment in the curriculum to a study of the Catholic tradition. But little will thereby be effected unless the faculty teaching religion and theology include at least some laymen, non-Catholics and even non-Christians. Courses in these areas must not appear to be monopolized by clerics or religious, especially when laymen are frequently academically more qualified. Non-Catholics are also necessary in order that the religious values of other traditions may to some small extent actually be seen by students as incarnated in a personal presence. A Catholic theological faculty should try to represent in microcosm all the theological currents operative in the Church as a whole. One of the miracles of the Council has been that these currents have become marvelously inclusive. The Catholic college should commit itself to this inclusiveness, for it is precisely here that it will manifest most the Church's embrace of the modern world.

We may bring to conclusion this effort to specify the role of theology by underlining once more the three points we have made: Courses concerning the religious dimension of man should be required of all college students if they are to be acquainted at a mature level with the total human achievement; no course in Catholic belief should be required of any Catholic student; the religious commitment of the Catholic, far from being weakened by such a policy, will find in it the necessary condition for development. Nor should there be any misgivings that Catholics under a program like this will somehow compare unfavorably with those of a former age. Those who fear this usually take as their norm external religious observance, which is a dubious yardstick for measuring anything today. For on the one hand the Church's liberation from the legalism of a past era has put external religious observance in its proper theological perspective, while on the other hand the absence of social sanction for such observance has forced decisions in this area to come more and more from the student's own interior conviction. Be that as it may, no one who has taught for any time in a Catholic college can avoid being impressed by the manifest goodness of students, their desire for what is authentic in religious experience and their rejection of all that fails to ring true. Ultimately it is not any course in Christian theology which is responsible for this, but the action of God at the center of a man or woman's life. In the end only he can produce the *metanoia* of the Gospels, the change of mind, the complete transformation in the human heart. Theology and religion, like every other intellectual discipline, must therefore regretfully subscribe to Newman's poignant lament: "Quarry the granite rock with razors, or moor the vessel with a thread of silk; then may you hope with such keen and delicate instruments as human knowledge and human reason to contend against those giants, the passion and pride of man." [9]

V

Woman in the Church

In *The Second Sex*, one of her most controversial books, Simone de Beauvoir insists that in spite of all that Christianity has done for women it has nonetheless contributed in no small measure to keeping her in a state of dependence unworthy of her dignity as a human being. Such an accusation does in fact touch the nerve center of a problem area which has become the concern of a number of theologians in recent years. What precisely is woman's vocation in the Church, and does it indeed differ from that of man? As yet there are no satisfying answers to these questions. Several veins of thought have been uncovered, however, which promise eventually to yield a more satisfying theology of woman than we have today, and in what follows we shall examine these briefly and reflect upon the possible lines of their future development.

Before we begin, however, we should recognize that one of the chief reasons for lack of any extensive theological reflection upon woman in the Roman Catholic Church is that until 1945 no significant papal statement had ever been made on the new status achieved by woman through the great social, scientific, economic and political upheavals of the present century.[1] This is not to say that the Popes before Pius XII were unconcerned about woman. They were indeed concerned, but almost all their pronouncements concerned the duties of woman in marriage and family life.[2] Between 1945 and his death, however, Pius XII faced for the first time the fact that, even though the natural vocation of woman may be to maternity and the home, the individual vocation of a modern woman in the Church may well be to play a special role in social and even political life. God may deliberately be placing modern woman in circumstances which force her to work outside family life precisely in order to accomplish through her an influence upon society which she alone can exert. A woman with such a vocation would have to possess the same professional training as that of a man in any given area of influence. Hence the equality between man and woman must be recognized not simply on the human level, but on the social and political level as well.[3]

The revolutionary nature of these early statements of Pius XII can be judged by the fact that, when he made them, the official status of woman in the Church still tended to reflect a mentality current in the centuries when canon law was being elaborated, namely a conviction of woman's weakness and especially of her lack of skill. Church law consequently tried to protect her from a brutal and disorganized world by providing her either with a husband or with a walled cloister.[4] But with Pius XII there came solicitude not for the weakness of woman but for her mission in the Church. In later pronouncements his emphasis falls on the fact that the Church needs woman just as much as it does man, in order to promote on the various levels of human culture the Christian ideals of peace, justice and human dignity.[5] Woman is to accomplish this new role, moreover, by cultivating those very qualities which are characteristic of her as a person. There is to be no question, therefore, of modifying in any way her personal makeup, for it is precisely by being what she is that she will help to offset that impersonalism which tends to impregnate the organizational structures of modern life. Significantly enough, all these ideas were touched upon to some extent by John XXIII in a 1960 address, and he surely echoed the feelings of modern woman three years later: "Since women are becoming ever more conscious of their human dignity, they will not tolerate being treated as inanimate objects or mere instruments, but claim, both in domestic and in public life, the rights and duties that befit a human person." [6] Nevertheless, Pope John's purpose was clearly to leave the development of these ideas to the theologians and it is to this subject that we turn now.

I

What have the theologians done with the problem of modern woman's mission in the Church? At the risk of oversimplification, we can distinguish three main lines of development. The first is a strong emphasis upon the primitive biblical concept of the couple. Man and woman were created for each other, to love each other and to perpetuate each other. The plan of God is that there be neither man nor woman alone, but a community of the two. This community is an image of the divine Community, just as man and woman are equally an exact image of God. God's unity in a trinity of Persons reflects itself in a human nature which is bisexual. It is Karl Barth who has in fact given this idea its most forceful formulation: only male and female together are man. To be created in God's image means to be created male and female; these are synonymous expressions in the Book of Genesis and they designate the mystery of the free "I-Thou" relationship within God's own personal life insofar as it has been communicated to man. All that is feminine must somehow be present in God just as all that is masculine. The biblical concept of the couple thus shows human nature to be a third transcendent dimension, a completion perceptible only by the eye of faith.[7] Moreover, since Christ is mediator of this revelation, we can see how the true function of the relationship between Christ and the Church sketched in Ephesians 5, 32 is that of intermediate archetype to introduce man and woman into the mystery of the Trinity. If they want to imitate God, the man-woman couple must model itself on the Christ-Church couple. The resemblance of the human couple to God, which is stated in Genesis 1, 27, thus constitutes them a mystery parallel to that of Christ and the Church.

But this same concept likewise enables us to speak of masculine and feminine not as opposites but as complementary metaphysical principles which are in fact part of every man and woman's life. Virility and femininity would thus be seen as two modes of being human, two modes of reflecting the nature and activity of God. There must be gentleness, sensitivity and compassion in man as well as in woman, since these qualities are somehow also divine; for the same reason woman must develop strength, initiative and firmness of will, and become the maker as well as the mother. Such a theological perspective has served to throw into strong relief the positive value of feminine qualities. Femininity can be treated as a good in itself; no longer simply a way of facing life with feeble resources and the need of protection, but an original and autonomous mode of finite existence, present in man as well as woman, though usually tending to dominate in the latter. Bisexuality consequently points in two directions in the religious sphere: backward to the mystery of creation in God's image, and forward to human participation in the redemptive mission of Christ. Whatever distinctive contribution woman must make to this redemptive mission, it is absolutely necessary that she make it precisely as woman.[8]

This brings us to the second contemporary development regarding woman's role in the Church, namely the sporadic attempts which have taken place to articulate what Gertrud von le Fort has called "the nuptial character of culture." This does not mean that there are to be no independent cultural achievements by woman alone, but such achievements will be the exception. What woman accomplishes in the world she will almost always accomplish as a companion to man, for it is as man's companion that she constitutes one of the polarities of human nature. To see this relationship solely in terms of marriage and generation is to grasp only half its responsibility, for whatever applies to new being in a biological sense applies also to new life produced by artistic or spiritual creation. Man and woman together are needed to build human society. Man can make no truly creative contribution to human culture without a response from woman, an active response, for woman's receptivity is not passive acceptance but an answer to man, the answer to a companion who inspires, encourages and fructifies. The receptivity of woman is therefore dependent upon her initiative as a person. She will receive from man only if she wishes to receive and to the extent that she so desires and freely chooses.[9]

The necessity of this companionship and cooperation of woman in man's cultural undertakings will be seen more clearly, perhaps, if we reflect upon the importance of the religious element in all truly human achievements. This element involves humility and a

reverence for the divine which is needed before man can participate fruitfully in the creative activity of God. Such reverence and
humility, say those who write in this vein, would seem to be more
characteristic of woman than man. It is woman who symbolizes
the free and loving submission of creature to Creator and is able
to inspire this surrender in those around her. She tends to transcend the role she plays in events rather than to overrate it, and
can see more easily in the complete web of human action the
creative presence of God. The feminine impetus thus means an
impulse toward reverence. Woman's collaboration enables man to
realize that his own creative impetus is in reality a movement toward cooperation with God, who usually chooses to remain silent
in man's labor and in some sense anonymous. This creative
anonymity of God tends to be reflected in the active receptivity of
woman, and man must somehow participate in this receptivity if
he is to have reverence for God in the midst of his human
achievement.[10]

A third development in contemporary theology has been suggested by the evolutionary system of Pierre Teilhard de Chardin.
Teilhard was convinced that true evolutionary progress resides not
in the forces of tangential energy, now moving inevitably toward
an ever greater technical mastery of mind over matter, but rather
in the forces of radial energy, which in man have become "psy-
chosocial," urging him forward toward ever higher forms of interpersonal communion. Because modern man has suddenly become
conscious of what is taking place in him, it follows that the successful outcome of evolution now depends upon his free decision
to cooperate with these forces of radial energy which, in Teilhard's
system, reach their highest form in human love. Love is in fact the
key to the whole evolutionary process, since it alone unites human
beings in such a way as to complete and fulfill them by joining
them to what is deepest in themselves. On the strictly phenomenological level this is a fact of daily experience, especially in the
sexual love between husband and wife, and in several of his
essays Teilhard goes out of his way to discuss this "sexual sense"
in relationship to what he calls the growth of amorization in the
noosphere.[11]

This love between man and woman, however, can have no

lasting significance for the human race unless it conquer the temptation to create "a universe for two" and submit to a growth by which the "sexual sense" is gradually transformed into a human and cosmic sense. Teilhard's faith in Christian revelation, moreover, enabled him to link this growth of love energy to the growth of Christian charity, since in the present supernatural order the real Omega of evolution is the Body-Person of Christ. Christ is the Center toward which all true love and charity must converge; in him alone will the married couple find that equilibrium necessary for an unselfish expansion of their human love toward the community and the world. "Love is a function of three terms: man, woman and God. Its whole perfection and success is bound up with the balanced harmony of these three elements." [12]

We must recognize, therefore, that human love is still in process of development. As an energy it goes far beyond the needs of reproduction and is searching ceaselessly for fuller and more meaningful forms of expression. Woman has not yet completely revealed man to himself, nor vice versa. It is not in isolation that man and woman move toward God; the evolving structure of the universe demands that these two modalities of human nature progress upward together. To divorce the spiritual progress of mankind from relationships between the sexes, whether in or outside marriage, is to forget that this duality must eventually be found even when human nature is completely divinized and united to Christ at the end of time. Spiritual aspiration cannot be based on the human "monad," but only on the human "dyad."

Now for Teilhard woman is the key to this development of the human dyad, because she is, much more than man, eminently suitable to be the carrier of unselfish love, and hence a factor of balance and equilibrium. It is through her that the action of Christ will usually pass in sublimating sexual attraction. "For man, woman is the one term capable of launching this forward movement. Through woman and through woman alone is man able to escape the isolation in which he risks becoming imprisoned by reason of his own masculine perfection." [13] Because the feminine influence tends to arouse and to nourish a love of the invisible, Teilhard sees this influence as the basis of woman's vocation in the world. "No man can do without the feminine, any more than he can do without light, oxygen or vitamins, and the evidence for this becomes more glaring every day." [14] Woman thus becomes in Teilhard's system the affective principle in cosmic development, the symbol of a world in evolution, the unifying impetus by which the human race is enabled to take the step toward universal love.

II

The three veins of thought we have just examined show promise of yielding a more satisfying theology of woman than we have today, and a brief reflection is now in order regarding possible lines of future development. One of these may well come from the concerted theological effort today to bring Mariology closer to its Christological center and to present doctrine concerning Mary in the context of her relationship to the Church. The Dogmatic Constitution on the Church of Vatican II has in fact attempted to do this by making Mary's motherhood the fundamental fact in interpreting all statements concerning her role as mediatrix in the economy of salvation. Precisely because she is mother of Christ she cares for all the brethren of Christ. His unique office as Mediator, shared by all Christians insofar as they are helpers and mediators to each other, is shared in a special way by Mary, just as his unique office as Priest is shared at different levels by his ministers. Mary cooperates in the work of salvation, therefore, in the same way as every Christian does, through faith, charity and union with Christ; and if she is rightfully considered to be the type or image of the Church, this is because her cooperation was perfect and her union with Christ complete.[15]

This insistence today upon Mary's active role in the Church as a function of her motherhood may well become the starting point for some meaningful theological resolution of that dilemma so painful to modern woman, namely, the dichotomy between freedom and femininity. The clarification of doctrine is always in God's providence a response to definite religious dangers, and one of these is certainly the future of contemporary woman. In the past she has been faced with a vast historical heritage of prejudice and custom, which forced her to keep well outside the masculine world and made her quite incapable of cooperating in any meaningful way with man's decisions and achievements. The danger now is that, in order to possess that complete equality with man which seems at last within reach, she will want to become more and more like man and less and less like woman. Such a tendency is in fact just as destructive as its opposite extreme, which seeks to chain woman to an abstract "nature" or to imprison her in a highly elaborated set of "feminine" qualities which discourage her initiative and ignore her originality as a person. What is needed then is an equilibrium, and this could well come from a deeper understanding of Mary's relationship to Christ and the Church. For Mary is the eternal woman in a truly ontological sense, and every woman becomes more like her insofar as she fulfills her mission in life, whether she herself is psychologically conscious of this or not. Mary's cooperation with God's plan for the world today is an active mediatorial effort, for she shares this office of her Son at its highest level. Yet she is mediatrix always as mother, with that tenderness which motherhood brings. Woman has need for such tenderness today, certainly as much as she has for autonomy, and her new-found freedom may itself be a silent plea that the tenderness of Mary be not excluded from the mechanized world of tomorrow.

A second line of development in the theology of woman may come when Catholic women are eventually allowed a greater voice in the decision-making of the Church. It has been said often enough, and not without reason, that in no institution in Western civilization is there less equality to be found between the sexes than in the Roman Catholic Church. To a large extent social and cultural reasons are responsible for this. Until modern times women have generally been thought incompetent in public affairs, and we have already seen to what extent canon law was influenced by this mentality. While always maintaining the equality of woman with man in their relationship with God (in accordance with Galatians 3, 28: "There is neither male nor female . . . in Christ Jesus"), ecclesiastical authority said almost nothing of their relationships in Church life. It is true that over the centuries great authority had been exercised by women who founded and governed various religious orders, but such authority had never been extended beyond these groups into the hierarchical and parochial functioning of the Church. Hence the immense irony in a statement of the Second Vatican Council which fails to mention this Church problem at all: "In truth it must still be regretted that fundamental personal rights are not yet being universally honored. Such is the case of a woman who is denied the right and freedom to choose a husband, to embrace a state of life, or to acquire an education or cultural benefits equal to those recognized for men." [16]

This brings us now to the much more fundamental reason for excluding women from any kind of direction in Church affairs: the various levels of this direction have always been associated historically with the priesthood. As a consequence, the question of whether women may be ordained priests has now become the focal point for the whole discussion of man-woman relationship in the Church. From the most primitive times in fact women have been excluded from such ordination, although no intrinsic doctrinal reason has ever been adduced against it, either from Scripture or the nature of woman, but only historical conditions of time and place.[17] The order of deaconess, moreover, which was flourishing in the Church by the third century, most likely went back to apostolic times and clearly seems to have involved a genuine sacramental ordination. These women preached and even distributed Holy Communion, although their primary function seems to have been to teach and exercise authority in charitable works.[18] No feminine clergy ever seems to have developed, however, and liturgical customs very soon excluded women altogether from any official function at the Eucharistic celebration. Though they were recognized, by reason of baptism, to be participants in the priesthood of Christ at the level common to all the faithful, only men were ever ordained to the official priesthood.

But must all future discussion of an equal voice for women in the Church center upon the priesthood? What modern woman really wants is for her voice to be heard in ecclesiastical affairs; very few indeed are interested in ecclesiastical careers. Nor does it take much insight to realize that becoming a priest is precisely the way to lose one's voice and most likely be prevented from influencing any decision. The question of woman's place in cult, therefore, is really a secondary question, pushed into the limelight as the chief means just now of testing the principle of equality. Ordaining women priests as a result of mere agitation, prescinding from whether such a step would be a natural outgrowth of need and the demands of a changing theology of ministry, would in fact be a very bad thing for the Church and secure relatively little benefit to women. Giving woman an ecclesiastical voice, however, by reason of her participation not in Christ's priestly or kingly function but in his function as prophet, is an entirely different question. Restoration of the primitive office of deaconess would be the most striking step in this direction, especially if such an office carried with it a certain degree of authority. Certainly until *some* public ecclesiastical position is actually conferred upon *some* women, it is difficult to see how the Church can claim that her male and female members enjoy the same equality they enjoy in civil society.

Far more important than the office of deaconess, however (which would likely involve an ecclesiastical career), would be an official Church policy to have women on all advisory boards in parishes as well as in dioceses. This would make it obvious to all that women were being consulted by right and not by suffrance, and that they were in a position publicly to exercise their prophetic or teaching function on all the various parish and diocesan levels. Nor can it be objected here (as it frequently is) that St. Paul did not favor such a role for women. His clear affirmation of equality in Galatians 3, 28 refutes this. For it is obvious that he would tend to give specific injunctions within the context of the Hellenic world of the time, as well as in the context of his strong affirmation of equality before God in Galatians 3, 28. The passage in 1 Timothy 2, 8-15, for example, clearly mixes admonitions of silence for women with prescriptions regarding clothes and other social customs, and it is difficult to see how any part of the passage could be other than human advice. In 1 Corinthians 11, 3-16, the context is clearly one of woman's right to pray in the public assembly and also to preach under certain conditions; Paul speaks of her subordination in the social order because he could speak no other way. The injunction of 1 Corinthians 14, 34, on the other hand

("Let the women keep silent in the meetings"), most likely concerns ordinary members of the congregation and not the "preaching" women whose rights Paul has vindicated in Chapter 11. The silence involved is in contrast to "asking questions," rather than to preaching, teaching or prophesying. The occasion for the prohibition seems to have been the custom at Corinth to have discussions following the reading of Scripture. In verses 16-33 Paul gives rules of decorum to be observed at these times, and in verses 34-35 he goes on to silence wives who, contrary to Jewish and Greek custom, wished to take part in the question period. No one can legitimately invoke such a prohibition today, however, when women who speak in public shock no one at all.[19]

Most of what has been said thus far is actually part of a much larger question, namely the relationship in the Church between Christians who have received the sacrament of orders or have entered religious life and those who have not. And here we find the third line of development in the current attempt to specify woman's vocation in the Church. For the ultimate reason for the lack of a serious theology of Christian woman is that up to now there has been no serious theology of Christian man. That is to say, there has been no serious effort to spell out a Christian anthropology which would make clear the relationship of the Christian *as person* to the various structures of human life. Nor is it difficult to see the reason for this. Karl Rahner has noted that before the advent of the modern world the only things that could really interest a man intellectually and absorb him, over and above the satisfaction of the most immediate requirements of life, were religious questions of human existence. Whatever else there was, like art and science, was itself a moment of the religious question. Hence the main preoccupation of the Church was with the role of hierarch, priest and religious (since these concerned themselves directly with the religious question) rather than with the role of Christian man as such. In contemporary life, however, the religious question has become one aspect only of human existence, and for many people not a very important one. Innumerable other factors call for man's interest and attention. Art, science, technology, politics, economics, all these have goals that are not "religious" at all. There now exists a world which man himself has brought forth out of nature, and the contemporary religious question is whether all the various elements of this world can be experienced in such a way that their Christian significance is not buried or lost.[20]

The contemporary situation has, then, resulted in a completely new meaning for the "lay" apostolate which it did not possess before. For the layman's role is to use the world *qua* world as the material for Christian existence, and this world has now become infinitely more complicated, interesting and subject to man's control. The two dimensions of Christian existence which have been sanctified by the sacraments of confirmation and matrimony, namely the family and public life, must therefore be redeemed in ways very different from those of former ages. This will not be done, obviously, by propaganda of any type or by trying to muffle every profane activity with religious overtones, but simply by the example given to others of living as a Christian in all the dimensions of the human. The Christian layman as such has no apostolic duty beyond this. Anything further would mean his sharing in the apostolates of the hierarchy, priest or religious. He is thus differentiated from these not as far as the ultimate goal and object of his apostolate are concerned, but only in regard to the *way* he is called upon to achieve it. And it is this "way" which still needs very serious theological attention.[21] Until it has been given, it is hardly possible to see with any clarity whether it can be broken down into a male and female "way." A secular career outside the home is becoming more and more important for the American woman, even if this is only a part-time involvement in professional life. Will her role as a Christian here really be different from that of the Christian male? The whole notion, moreover, of Christian involvement in the temporal is senseless unless there is serious concern for prayer and the interior life. For only insofar as one is united to Christ in love and friendship can one be a witness to him among one's fellow men. But does this mean that Christian spirituality must develop a distinctively masculine and feminine style? In the past the Church has been accused with good reason of being "effeminate" and "womanly" in its piety. While this is hardly a problem today, the question itself highlights once more this third line of development we have been considering: the theology of woman must be seen as a function of the larger question of the role of lay people in the Church.

III

The three lines of development we have outlined here are not the only ones possible. One area of neglect has certainly been the recognition of woman as a person. The present theological concern for freedom and interpersonal communion ought therefore to make more meaningful all future discussion of women. A thorough reevaluation of the current theology of sex and marriage would without doubt also bring rich insights.[22] It may well be asked, too, whether anyone but a woman will be able to make any original contribution to this area. Mary Daly's book *The Church and the Second Sex* is a good example of what a professional theologian can do with this problem from a woman's point of view. "What is needed," she writes toward the end of her perceptive study, "is creative effort to develop a theological anthropology which will study the dynamics of human personality and social relationship from a radically evolutionary point of view. Within this context there needs to be developed a theology of the man-woman relationship which rejects as alienating to both sexes the idea of a sexual hierarchy founded upon 'nature' and defined once and for all. This much needed theology will recognize that the relationship between the sexes evolves, that its forms must change according to the conditions of diverse historical epochs and according to individual differences. . . . It will be honest enough to admit the ambiguity of concrete reality, which the theologian's abstractions cannot fully clarify or encompass." [23]

One thing, therefore, is certain: up to now theology has neglected woman. Outside of a concern for family life, the Church has paid little attention to woman's personal mission and showed scant interest in giving her true equality with man in the affairs of parish or diocese. Certain also is the fact that this neglect must end. It is no longer feasible for Church leaders to profess an abstract ideology of equality and at the same time refuse to translate this into practical terms. Perhaps the saddest aspect of this situation is that the emancipation of women in the West can legitimately be regarded as a genuine development of the New Testament teaching on the freedom and dignity of the human person. What Krister Stendahl refers to as the "breakthrough" of Galatians 3, 28 was Paul's realization that being a Christian transcends not simply the historical and social categories of Jew/ Greek and slave/free, but even the biological distinction between men and women. The thinking of the Church needs desperately to catch up with the thinking of the contemporary world on woman's place in society. All aspects of woman's Christian vocation must in the future be accounted for, and the divine idea of which she is the realization must be brought right to the surface of the Christian consciousness, so that its riches may be seen at last and all its depth understood.

VI

Ignatian Spirituality Today

The unfortunate dichotomy between theology and spirituality, so widespread until recent years, has of late shown signs of disappearing once and for all. This has been a boon to both theologians and spiritual directors, since the previous separation frequently resulted in sterile theology and in spirituality nourished for the most part by will power or sentimentality. The present *rapprochement* has, moreover, provided an occasion for the various spiritualities in the Church to reexamine their origins as well as their own proper relationship to current theological development. In regard to Ignatian spirituality this has been going on for some time, especially in France and Germany. In English-speaking countries, however, this particular form of Christian spirituality still seems to be subject to a certain degree of misunderstanding, most of all in its relationship to new emphases in systematic and pastoral theology. Consequently it would not be out of place to summarize here the broad lines that distinguish the spirituality of St. Ignatius, and then to inquire into its valididty today when placed in the context of modern theological thought.

I

In a broad sense Christian spirituality may be defined as the way to holiness, that is to say, to man's full possession by the Father through Christ in the Spirit. In this broad understanding of the term there can be only one spirituality, since the one Way to holiness must always be the Person of Christ, and must lead always through his Church, his sacraments, his prayer, his virtues,

97

his grace. These are the general means of union with God which are common to all Christians. When, however, these general means become specific and are applied concretely in the lives of individual men and women, there necessarily results a certain style of approach to God, and it is this style of approach which is commonly termed a "spirituality" in the strict sense of the word. What is ultimately responsible for different styles of approach to God? The personality of the individual certainly, for in one sense it is true to say that each must have his own spirituality. While every Christian must indeed make an effort to live out the whole of the Gospel, still each is limited as a man, and the lines of the structure which grace erects must somehow be obedient to what nature provides. The grace that each one receives is uniquely his own and consequently his response must likewise be uniquely personal. John Courtney Murray said well that God would have each man wholly his witness, but not necessarily a witness to the whole of him. Only the Church, as the community of the faithful, in her many-splendored variety, is a witness to the whole counsel of God.

But there is a second and more fundamental reason for different spiritualities in the Church, and this is the challenge of society at any given time and place in history.[1] These challenges to the Church at the crucial turning points in history have, in God's providence, brought forth mighty responses from certain extraordinary men and women. So penetrating is their vision of the relevance of Christianity to a given age, that they are followed by large numbers of Christians who wish to share this vision, and consequently "schools" of spirituality form. The Benedictine, Dominican and Carmelite schools, for example, all sprang from definite needs of the Church at a given historical period. Such a school of spirituality will contain both a vision and a technique. The vision, the particular response to a particular grace of the Holy Spirit, will be permanent; the technique, the point of contact of the vision with the needs of a given age, will be fluid and will change as society itself changes. Thus we may more accurately define a spirituality in a strict sense as the form or style of a person's response to the grace of Christ before the challenge of daily living in a society environment.

We are now in a position to examine the vision of one of these extraordinary men in the Church, Ignatius Loyola, and to see its relevance as a response to the challenge of the society in which he lived. The pattern of Renaissance life in sixteenth-century Europe had come to base itself more and more on individualism and independence, on emotionalism and subjectivity. In the political and religious order there was incipient revolt from authority in all its forms. Private judgment was elevated into an absolute and became the sole standard and norm for all decisions. Among the educated and ignorant alike there was the cult of humanism, which made personal satisfaction almost a fetish and luxurious living alone the symbol of the fully human life. This was, unfortunately, the case even among the clergy, where worldliness and ignorance combined in a strange mixture of extremes which could not help but be reflected in the lives of Christian people as a whole. There was, moreover, the discovery of the New World, opening up limitless horizons not only for military and commerical enterprises but also for the coming of the Kingdom of Christ. Yet blocking the way to this dynamic missionary effort was the corruption that had crept into the Church herself. A lethargy was hanging over the Church like a pall, while under it ran a deeper and deeper current of anxiety among spiritually-minded men everywhere for a genuine and permanent reform.

In the face of this challenge the grace of God inspired Ignatius Loyola with both a vision and a practical technique. The technique does not concern us here, since that which is permanent and enduring in the Ignatian legacy to the Church is his vision of the Christian life. At the risk of oversimplification we shall say that this distinctive vision is made up of an interior and an exterior aspect. What may be called its interior aspect consists in an emphasis on the element of choice in the spiritual life. This originated ultimately in Ignatius' own profound experience at the time of his conversion, and it has lodged itself permanently in his Spiritual Exercises as their whole purpose and *raison d'être*. Such an emphasis is aimed at fostering a disposition of soul by which one is able to choose, under the guidance of the Spirit of Christ and opposed to the spirit of evil, that concrete course of action which God wishes here and now for his greater glory.

It should not be difficult to see how insistence on this seemingly simple formulation went to the very heart of the needs and abuses in the Church of the sixteenth century. Utilizing the individualistic tendency of the age, Ignatius underlined the need for personal choice in prayer, the purpose of which is to center a man on God, the goal of his whole existence, who alone can lay claim to all man's praise, reverence and service. To a society becoming more and more infected with exaggerated spiritual subjectivity, Ignatius pointed to the need for objectivity in prayer, namely the need to discover God's plan for one's life, not to make up a plan of one's own. To an age accustomed to the glory and grandeur of earthly kings, Ignatius proclaimed that all God's glory is centered in the kingly Person of Christ, who calls each man to enter into personal companionship with him. Only by being united in love and service with the Incarnate Son does a man gain strength and courage to direct his life to the glory of the Father. Attachment to Christ is alone the source of detachment from self.

Hence for St. Ignatius there is no question whatsoever of these choices for God's glory coming as a result of natural energy of character or some self-centered ascetic discipline. The human effort he insisted upon had its source always in prayer and the grace of Christ given to each man through the action of the Holy Spirit. Dependence of the soul on the grace of the Holy Spirit is absolute. It is of the highest importance to see this as central in the mind of St. Ignatius. No one was more convinced than he that we can perform no good action unless we receive that good action as a gift from God. The need for humility is therefore self-evident. We can receive from God only if we admit our poverty and our need, and acknowledge that he alone can satisfy them. This is the true meaning of the frequently misunderstood "more" of Ignatian spirituality, the *magis,* by which Ignatius searched always for God's greater glory. This "more" of our generosity toward God can never be equated with any self-confident effort on our part. Rather, as St. Ignatius himself said, it is an attitude of mind by which "we are more and more eager to receive God's gifts," and by which we are enabled to unite "his greater service and our greater repose." [2]

Finally, for members of the Church of the sixteenth century, clergy and laity alike, girding themselves to battle against the enemies of the Church without, Ignatius insisted that the real foe was spiritual and that any campaign against him must begin in the heart of the individual. The figure of Christ on the cross, whom the retreatant meets so often in the course of the Spiritual Exercises, stands as God's own witness to the terrible destructive power of sin. But, even more, it stands as the symbol of Christ's victory, for the power of sin is personal, and on Calvary it was with this spirit of evil that Christ locked himself in mortal combat. The crucifix for St. Ignatius is indeed the supreme proof of Christ's love, but this love of Christ is a triumphant love which leads to the resurrection, a pledge of certain victory for every Christian who battles manfully against the spirit of evil in his own heart. Only when the good and evil spirits are polarized is one able to share in the joy of Christ's triumph and to see in his own life that course of action which is here and now for God's greater glory.

It is within this context of Christ's victory and the discernment of spirits in one's life that devotion to Mary finds its proper place in Ignatian spirituality. At all the critical choices of the Exercises the retreatant is asked to pray to Mary first before going to Christ and to the Father. This triple ascent is, of course, characteristic of the Church's prayer as a whole, but it is found here in a specifically Ignatian context. The divine economy operates from God to Christ through Mary to the apostle, and consequently the Christian is able to choose what is now for God's glory to the extent that he achieves what Christ achieved, complete surrender to the mystery of Mary's motherhood. It is she who brings him courage in his resolutions and grace to discern the spirits in himself and in the world about him, for as his Queen she is all-powerful with her Son. All spiritual growth means an imitation of Mary's *fiat,* so important for Christ's ultimate victory, by which she allowed God to operate freely in her life and so enabled the Word to become incarnate.

The first aspect of Ignatian spirituality is, then, an interior disposition of soul by which one's union with Christ and responsiveness to the movements of his spirit are oriented toward action which is here and now for God's greater glory. If we turn now to what may be called the exterior aspect, we shall see that it consists in a certain mode of exteriorizing this interior element of choice. How for St. Ignatius was this docility to the Spirit of Christ to be manifested concretely? His answer was quite clear: by a loving service of the Church, by ceaseless labor for whatever were her immediate needs. For in the case of the apostle it is precisely this ceaseless and unselfish labor which detaches him from himself, centers him more and more on Christ and through him on the Trinity, and in so doing becomes itself an exercise of prayer and contemplation. In this formulation is contained both the characteristic Ignatian devotion to the Church and the likewise characteristic "contemplation in action." Again, it was the challenge of the sixteenth century which evoked this double manifestation of an interior spirit. Ignatius was in his own way as much a revolutionary as any Protestant, but for him the phrase "Church militant," far from connoting a military attitude toward an opponent, meant rather the attitude which members had toward proper authorities and toward one another, the attitude of disciplined service for the Church.[3]

This orientation of Ignatian spirituality toward ceaseless labor eventually produced a challenge of its own, that which came to the life of prayer from a life of action. Ignatius' strong emphasis on action in the service of the Church would seem to involve a de-emphasis on prayer and therefore a deemphasis on the source of all fruitful action, God himself. Ignatius' reply was that both prayer and work, done according to God's will, are basically two aspects of a single thing: love. An apostle loves God precisely by "seeking the presence of God in all things, speaking, walking, listening, eating, working."[4] This type of prayer, says St. Ignatius, is better than hours of formal prayer and is also more difficult, since it demands greater self-abnegation. Yet it is capable of extending one's love in very wide circles and of developing an interior attitude of unselfish joy in following the flow of God's will in all creatures and situations. "There is more virtue and happiness in being able to enjoy the possession of the Lord in the midst of various works and places than in being alone with him."[5]

Since in the life of the apostle, therefore, the time of formal prayer must be limited, the prayer itself must be seen not as an end, as in the contemplative life, but as a means, disposing the apostle to accomplish the will of God with greater fidelity. An example of this is the paramount importance of the examination of conscience in the spirituality of St. Ignatius. Far from being a petty cataloging of faults or exercise in introspection, it was intended by him primarily as a turning toward Christ in love and companionship to examine the decisions made and to be made for him during the day. It is a prayer in which God's light is allowed to fall upon all the selfishness and frailty of mixed motives by which the movement of one's action toward God has been deflected into ambiguity. It is a prayer of confidence and trust. Above all it is a prayer in which one becomes present to all the needs of the neighbor and to whatever choices God wishes made here and now in regard to those needs. Such a directing of formal prayer toward action in service of the neighbor has as its corollary that action itself should not only lead to true prayer and greater love, but should actually *be* these insofar as the apostle unselfishly seeks therein the will of God. This is "contemplation in action," giving conscious preference to apostolic interests over selfish interests, to God's plans over human plans, and in so doing to possess in the midst of action an awareness of the presence of God which is the very essence of contemplative prayer.[6]

II

The distinctive character of Ignatian spirituality, which we have sketched just now under what may be called its interior and exterior aspects, took its origin primarily as a response to the challenge of the sixteenth century. Yet this legacy of St. Ignatius to the Church, so unmistakably valid for the world of his time, has a new and equally unmistakable validity today precisely because of the recent developments in systematic and pastoral theology. These modern emphases are serving now to deepen even more the primordial Ignatian concepts and to give to his vision of the Christian life a new and even richer dimension. This may perhaps be seen more clearly if we first briefly situate these main theological currents against the background of secular thought.

The thoughtful man's outlook on life in the twentieth century has been decisively influenced by three converging movements, three challenges symbolized by the names of the challengers, Darwin, Marx and Freud. From Charles Darwin has come the discovery of cosmic and organic evolution, commonly considered one of the greatest achievements of the human mind, a discovery which has brought man to a consciousness of the unity of the human species never before possible on the natural level. From Karl Marx has come a reinterpretation of all history in terms of economics, which has resulted in focusing attention on the dynamic aspects of historical change as well as on the crying need for social reform in every area of society. Finally, from Sigmund Freud has come what Karl Stern calls the third revolution, the discovery of the subconscious, that mysterious dimension of the human personality which has generated such an uncommon interest today in man's interior psychological states.

The mentality which produced these scientific developments could not help but register as well in areas of theological thought. The new concept of the natural universe as a huge organism growing toward maturity found its parallel on the supernatural level in the doctrine of the Church as the living and developing Body of Christ, growing toward final maturity at the end of time. This manner of conceiving the Church, which lay dormant since the time of Paul and Augustine, has now come into its own as a major theological concern, and has given to theology as a whole a distinctly ecclesiological perspective. This has been intensified by the modern liturgical renaissance, which points to the Eucharist as both the symbol and reality of the Church, where the whole of God's people are united with the Person of Christ as well as with one another in public worship.

Other theological developments have been even more significant. The scientific study of Sacred Scripture has revitalized the very concept exploited so effectively by Karl Marx, namely the Christian concept of history as a dynamic force moving toward a preconceived end, understood in terms of the Church and the living Person of Christ. The personal interventions of God into human history, recorded in the Bible in all their magnitude, show history itself to be the stage upon which God works out his designs. This rediscovery of the biblical outlook on man has had its counterpart also in the social order, where there has been strong emphasis on the Christian's obligation to society as well as a serious theological inquiry into the real meaning of Christian work. On the part of the Catholic layman this has been accompanied by an emerging consciousness of his own identity, as well as his function in the Church and the nature of his apostolate.

Lastly, as a result of present-day concern for the person, there has opened up a field of theological investigation which promises to make abundant use of all the resources of modern psychiatry, namely the relationship between grace and human personality. Already the study of the mechanisms of free decision has given new meaning to the Church's teaching that grace tends toward the perfection and not the repression of human freedom. Theologians even speak today of a "psychology of grace." Rich veins of insight have come to light, moreover, regarding the indwelling of the Holy Spirit and his role in causing grace, and especially regarding the personal relationship which the Christian has to each of the three divine Persons. For centuries this doctrine has remained in the background, yet perhaps no other truth of revelation has so affected the spiritual life in our time or so influenced the Christian's attitude toward prayer and sacramental symbolism.

What have these modern developments in secular and religious thought to do with St. Ignatius' vision of the Christian life? It will be recalled that we described its interior aspect as an emphasis on choosing for God's greater glory, and its exterior aspect as a manifestation of this interior disposition through loving service of the Church. The answer here proposed, therefore, is that each of these modern developments has been serving in its own way to deepen one or other of these two aspects of Ignatius' vision. Its interior aspect, first of all, has been very strongly affected by the rediscovery and reemphasis of the great biblical themes of salvation. Nowhere is the discernment of spirits thrown into sharper relief than in the pages of the New Testament. There Christ's whole work of redemption is presented as a conflict with the spirit of evil and ultimate victory over the forces of sin, suffering and death, a victory for all men, since all were present in Christ. But while the evangelists and St. Paul paint this conflict on the immense canvas of salvation history, in the mind of St. Ignatius the field of battle is the individual soul. For him the decisive combat won on Calvary must be fought again in the recesses of the human heart, where Christ meets his adversary anew in every effort of man to purify himself, his motives, his attitudes. It is this interior struggle, so crucial in all spiritual and apostolic decisions, which today has taken on a perspective that is properly biblical and salvific.

The renewed interest in the relationship of grace to human freedom has also influenced this interior aspect. This has been due in large part to modern psychiatry's investigation of those non-voluntary dynamisms which are part of every personality. Infraconscious and of multiple dimensions, they are not juxtaposed but integrated into one's freedom of choice. Because man is a unity, his free decisions do not exist apart from these dynamisms, but take shape precisely by using the energies contained on this non-voluntary level. Such "using" of one's dynamisms, either accepting or rejecting them, depends to a great extent on one's self-knowledge as well as on the values one intends to pursue. In this context the Ignatian stress on discernment of spirits, docility to the Spirit of Christ and pursuit of God's greater glory, takes on a new significance. Self-examination becomes much less a preoccupation with oneself and much more a movement into reality, an acquiescence to the action of grace which penetrates to all areas of one's personality. This divine initiative, operating as it does on the level of the subconscious as well as the conscious, is what progressively liberates the Christian to choose the good, to achieve inner balance, to act with confidence and to become his true self.

The divinization of the Christian in sanctifying grace has been a third source of enrichment to this interior aspect of Ignatian spirituality. Much of what we are achieving today through an intense study of theology St. Ignatius seems to have achieved by sudden insight and extraordinary mystical graces, enabling him to be almost uninterruptedly conscious of the presence of the Blessed Trinity. A record of these graces still exists in the few fragments we have of his spiritual journal, where the decisions he made in the daily government of his Society are continually referred to the three Persons for their ratification and approval.[7] Indeed, his journal and autobiography, which are no less important than the Spiritual Exercises for an understanding of his spirituality, show his whole orientation in prayer to be essentially Trinitarian.[8] That this was never made more explicit in the Exercises themselves is due most likely to the Saint's natural disposition toward action rather than speculative thought, and also to the fact that scholastic theology at the time was much more interested in grace as a created quality received from God than as a bond which united each man personally to the divine Persons. Yet the key concepts of his spirituality all take on a new meaning in the light of the divine indwelling. Even one's sorrow for sin, that sense of being abashed at one's infidelity to God, so important in the early part of the Exercises, becomes an acknowledgment of the baseness of the vessel into which the three Persons come to dwell as in a temple.

Modern theological developments have likewise had their effect upon the exterior aspect of St. Ignatius' spirituality, his loving service of the Church. This is true, first of all, of the doctrine of the Church as Body of Christ and the modern liturgical movement so closely connected with it. St. Ignatius was far from being ignorant of his doctrine, but there is a stark contrast between its general neglect in his lifetime and the rich development given to it by the Church today. As a result, his passionate devotion to the Church was centered on her more as an institution than as a community. The same is true of the liturgy: the rebirth and growth of a sense of community worship is a relatively recent phenomenon. St. Ignatius' liturgical sense must therefore be judged by the liturgical sense which the Church herself possessed in the sixteenth century. It is well known, for example, how much importance the Saint attached to frequent communion and how much his followers were responsible for the restoration of this practice. He himself eventually had to be forbidden to read the breviary because its recitation brought such a flood of tears that there was danger of its destroying his sight. "If I had followed my own inclination," he told another Jesuit, "I would have had choir and chant in the Society; but I did not do so because God our Lord has given me to understand that it is not his will." [9]

Nowhere, however, is St. Ignatius' liturgical sense more clearly manifested than in the central place which the Eucharist held in his spiritual life. In the thirteen months covered by his spiritual journal we have a record of consolations, visions, illuminations, tears, almost all experienced during his celebration of the Eucharist, and this in the midst of an intensely active life. Even special graces received in the course of the day appear practically always as a prolongation or complement of those of the Eucharist. It was evidently the Eucharist which enabled him to achieve that extraordinary simplicity in his spiritual life, for it was there that he found everything, the whole source and support of his loving service of the Church. This Eucharistic orientation of his spirituality was basically an outgrowth of his tender love for Christ as Mediator, who in the Eucharist brings into concrete focus the whole of reality, God, man, the material universe. Such an orientation is reason enough for asserting that for him there would be immediate appeal in the modern conception of the Church as Body of Christ and people of God united in public worship.

The Second Vatican Council emphasized strongly the complementary nature of public and private prayer, and their need for mutual enrichment.[10] The relationship between the liturgy and the Spiritual Exercises is a clear example of this, since they each draw their substance from the same source: salvation history. The liturgy presents the great events of Christ's life in a more leisurely way, harmonizing them slowly with the year's whole cosmic cycle. An Ignatian retreat, on the other hand, telescopes these same mysteries into a much shorter period, a month or less. In neither case, however, can the events of salvation history be considered as actions merely of the past. The Christ of St. Ignatius as well as of the liturgy is the risen Christ, living now in his Church and continuing his work of salvation until the Parousia. The very concentration of the Exercises is able to bring this home with greater force. The events of the liturgical year, consequently, should have a deeper personal meaning for one who has lived through them in the silence of a retreat, while liturgical prayer should have the salutary effect of guarding one's private prayer from sentimentality and introspection. It is this common bond between the liturgy and the Exercises which enables each in its own way and on its own level to foster the growth of Christ in all the members of his Body.[11]

The second major enrichment to this exterior aspect of service in the Church has come from the modern phenomenon of the lay apostolate. The layman has gradually become aware that he is, by his very definition, a Christian who lives in the world and is deeply involved in the work of the world. His proper function in the Church is not directly salvific, but is directed rather toward the temporal as such, toward the construction and reformation of human institutions. It is in this way that he shares in the creative and redemptive work of Christ. To be an intelligent mediator through whom the latent perfections of the universe are brought to fruition and offered back to God, this is to perform a task specifically Christian. So central is this mission of the layman that it once prompted Pius XII, in addressing the College of Cardinals, to give this remarkable definition of the Church: "Considered from this point of view [her mission to society], the Church may be called the assembly of those who, under the supernatural influence of grace, in the perfection of their personal dignity as sons of God and the harmonious development of all human inclinations and energies, build the powerful structure of human society." [12]

Such a broadened view of the Church and the layman's role has occasioned a totally new application of St. Ignatius' "*mystique* of service." Like Calvin he was obsessed with the idea of ceaseless labor, but in his spirituality work for the Church was inculcated as an exercise of love, a way of "finding God in all things." Now it is precisely within this context of service of the Church that the modern apostle faces the perennial challenge of action to the life of prayer. If he sees his proper work in the Church as a total engagement in the profane order, he soon realizes that formal prayer as a consequence must be strictly limited in his life, though his call to sanctity remains clear. He may well ask himself, moreover, whether work motivated by love does not change its whole relationship not only to God but also to one's personal dignity and development as a man. These and other considerations are becoming the primary concern for the nascent theology of work, and they point to the modern layman's felt need for a richer union of prayer and action. The *mystique* of service at the heart of Ignatian spirituality can make a positive contribution toward solving this need, and toward helping the action of the layman to become itself an exercise of the presence of God.

III

This chapter has had as its purpose briefly to situate the broad lines of the spirituality of St. Ignatius in relation to modern theology. It should be emphasized again that we have been discussing one particular form of the Christian life, characterized by distinctive historical origins and distinctive emphases in both prayer and the apostolate. The initial Ignatian vision was a spirituality of interior solitude and detachment from the world, and therefore a spirituality of the cross. As such it took its place in direct continuity with the main current of spirituality up to his time. But such solitude and detachment made sense for Ignatius only as a means to become more open to grace and more disposed to act for God's greater glory, for in his mind it was through action undertaken in service of the Church that holiness was essentially to be achieved. That which St. John of the Cross described so forcefully in his *Dark Night of the Soul* must take place also in the life of the apostle, but in his case this purification is accomplished in and through the apostolic action itself, its demands, its frustrations and its failures. Continual mortification is indeed necessary, but this never means disengagement or flight from the sensible. On the contrary, the ultimate aim of all formal prayer is to enable the Christian to find God in every creature, to love all creation as God himself does, positively, through activity.[13] Remaining always Trinitarian and Eucharistic in its orientation, Ignatian spirituality is a *mystique* of service through love rather than of loving union, in which the Person of Christ is the great Mediator between God, man and the material world. Developments in modern theological thought have been serving to uncover new meaning and insight in these primordial Ignatian concepts. The Saint himself, so keenly aware of challenges in the sixteenth century, would be the first to welcome this enrichment of his spirituality which has come from the challenges of today.

It would not be out of place, before we close, to add as a corollary a brief word on the delicate question of the relationship between formal prayer, apostolic work and union with God. For there will always be the danger of a false and overfacile identification of prayer and action, as well as the necessity for some measure of solitude and recollection in order to develop as a Christian. The mistake, however, is to think that the relation between formal prayer and action is really the same in both the spirituality of St. Ignatius and that of the contemplative life, the only difference being that apostolic activity characterizes the one and not the other. The usual presupposition here is that St. Thomas' definition of the "mixed life" as *contemplata aliis tradere* is equally applicable both to the apostolic life as conceived by St. Ignatius and to the monk forced by circumstances to engage in an apostolate. This is not so. However valid the concept of *contemplata tradere* may be, it is not Ignatian, for it identifies contemplation with formal prayer and sharply distinguishes it from apostolic action. "Contemplation" in the Ignatian sense corresponds not to formal prayer but to intimacy and union with God, and this is to be found not only in formal prayer but also in apostolic activity.

St. Ignatius thought it an imperfection that long hours of formal prayer should be needed to unite oneself to God. What he insisted upon was rather great detachment, a continual mortification of one's own interests and desires so that one's heart could be centered on God in the midst of work. In his mind union with God in formal prayer is to be ordered always to the greater perfection of one's union with God in action. This union with God in action has sometimes been called "virtual" prayer, and it is measured not by clarity of intellectual awareness but by the degree of one's self-forgetfulness and surrender to God. It is the virtual continuation of an actual desire to seek and find God in all things. "In all things let them seek God," said Ignatius, "withdrawing themselves as far as possible from all love of creatures, that they may put their whole affection on the Creator of them, loving him in all creatures and them in him." In Ignatian spirituality, therefore, the apostolic life is not a consequence of love for God but the form of it; Christian perfection in both its ascetical and mystical aspects is to be found essentially not in formal prayer but in apostolic action undertaken for the glory of God. Such a life is not a "mixed life" at all, but wholly an active one.

There is here no question whatsoever of deprecating contemplation in the monastic sense. What we are dealing with is a totally different vocation in the Church as well as a totally different style of approach to God. Nor do I wish in the least to suggest that Ignatian contemplation is any easier to achieve than that of the monastery. If anything it is more difficult. But there is such a thing as the grace of vocation as well as a gradual growth over the years in fidelity to that grace. Not everyone called to follow the Ignatian way to God reaches the perfection of contemplation in action, just as not everyone called to the monastery reaches the summit of contemplative prayer. Yet in each case it is the ideal which gives substance and direction to their lives and so constitutes the distinctive character of their respective spiritualities.

PART THREE
The Optic of Teilhard de Chardin

VII

Evolution and the Problem of God

In his book *No Other God,* Gabriel Vahanian notes with perceptive accuracy that "the vulnerability of the Christian faith hinges today on the fact that there can be no faith in God which does not assume a concomitant cultural obligation. There can be no faith without secularity. . . . Should, then, the Christian faith be unable to overcome its present cultural estrangement . . . its only alternative is to become an esoteric mystery cult, that is, the very antithesis of what it has claimed to be for twenty centuries." [1] What I wish to underline here is that a major preoccupation in the writings of Pierre Teilhard de Chardin is precisely to overcome the present cultural estrangement of the Christian faith. His efforts, made over a period of forty years and bridging two world wars, have in the course of time reflected the growing concern of an ever larger number of Christians. "The People of God," says the Second Vatican Council, "labors to decipher authentic signs of God's presence and purpose in the happenings, needs and desires in which this People has a part along with other men of our age. For faith throws a new light on everything, manifests God's design for man's total vocation, and thus directs the mind to solutions that are fully human. . . . This Council wishes to assess in this light those values which are most highly prized today, and to relate them to their divine source." [2]

No one surely was more conscious of these "happenings, needs, and desires" of our age than Teilhard de Chardin. Nor was anyone more anxious than he to find therein "authentic signs of God's presence and purpose," so that the unbeliever might see how

Christian faith "directs the mind to solutions which are fully
human." It was indeed through this double effort that he sought to
overcome the present cultural estrangement of Christianity, and he
developed as a consequence a dialectic on the problem of God
oriented toward the temporal as well as toward the eternal.
Nevertheless, it must be insisted upon that for Teilhard the
problem of God was initially a personal problem. What he always
fell back upon was his personal experience. It was this experience of a hidden God, who remains hidden even when
experienced, which convinced Teilhard that he had a message for
modern man. This message was a double one: man's need for an
absolute and man's need for Christ. These two needs Teilhard
had himself experienced in and through his commitment to
science and contemporary culture, and he believed that an analysis
of the evolutionary process could help modern man to recognize
these needs also in himself. To document, then, Teilhard's contribution to current discussion on the problem of God, we shall
briefly outline the problem as he experienced it personally and then
indicate how he developed his own double answer.

I

Everyone today is aware that Teilhard's fundamental problem
of life was a clarification of the relationship between the world
which he had discovered through science and the God whom he
had experienced through faith. He lived too close to the modern
unbeliever not to be vividly aware of the possibility of living a fully
human life without any concern for God at all. The humanist with
whom his scientific work brought him in daily contact inevitably
possessed a profound respect for the dignity of man, as well as an
enthusiasm for his exercise of freedom and his responsibility to
build a better world. His moral ideal, moreover, was usually
quite high, his dedication to his work total, and his commitment to
the values of technological progress sufficiently strong to motivate
his life. "There is a certain pessimism about," wrote Teilhard
once, "which keeps repeating that our world is sinking into atheism.
But shouldn't we rather say that what it suffers from is an un-

satisfied theism? You claim men no longer want God. But are you certain that what they are rejecting is not simply the image of a God too small to nourish our concern for survival and for a super-life, which is, after all, nothing else than our need to adore?" [3] And in another essay we find a remark which Teilhard said he had heard many times from unbelievers: "Were I to become a Christian, I feel I would be less a man." [4]

We accept as commonplace today that modern secular man finds it impossible to ask questions about God or Christianity in other than human terms. But Teilhard saw this clearly many years ago, at a time when it was recognized by relatively few Christians and admitted by almost none. "For a reason that is not clear," he wrote in 1949, "something in our time no longer 'clicks' between man and God, as God is presented to him today. Everything seems to point to the fact that man has no clear picture of the God he wants to adore. Hence the general impression . . . we get of an irresistible growth in atheism." [5] Such a growth, however, he felt to be only apparent. The heart of the problem was that God was now being experienced less in a religious and more in a cultural context. This was, he admitted, still an obscure experience, but nonetheless real and nonetheless to be valued. "Whatever reason there may be for condemning many of the forms taken by 'faith in the world,' these proceed from an undeniable effort to be loyal to life (that is to say, to God's creative action), and this we must respect." [6] Teilhard was conscious of having a very intense awareness of the aspirations deep at the heart of his age as other men seem to have of its miseries.[7] Destiny placed him, he said, at a privileged crossroads, where it was possible for him, in his double role as priest and man of science, to experience the interplay of two powerful currents, the one human and the other divine.[8] The following text, taken from an important essay written in 1934, makes this clear:

> After thirty years devoted to the pursuit of interior unity, I have the impression that at last a synthesis has taken place naturally between the two currents which draw me. Each has in turn strengthened not diminished the other. Today I probably believe more than ever in God, and certainly more than ever in the world. Is there not to be found here, on a small

scale and at least in rough form, the personal solution of the great spiritual problem which today confronts the vanguard of humanity? . . . Even understood in purely subjective terms, much of what I say must necessarily have an equivalent resonance even in temperaments unlike my own. Man is essentially one, and it is sufficient to go deep enough into oneself to find a single common ground of aspiration and insight.[9]

This last text makes it clear that Teilhard felt not only that his own problem was that of modern man generally, but also that his personal solution had, at least as a rough sketch, a universal validity. "The problem of God," he wrote, "today confronts the whole spectrum of human activity. We can come to grips with it only by using all the resources of research and human experience. Not only does God give a value to human effort which will last forever, but his revelation is precisely a response to the sum total of this effort." [10] In his own life, then, Teilhard had found a coherence between his faith in God and his faith in the world, and their meeting point was the broad support given by Christianity to human endeavor and to man's aspirations and hope for the future. At the core of his evolutionary system, consequently, we find a continuous effort to show that in the life and thought of Christianity we have the only religious organism capable of giving full meaning to the universe which man has discovered. And this is precisely the criterion of its truth as a religion, namely that through revelation "the world as a whole takes on a maximum of coherence for our intelligence and a maximum of appeal to our taste for action." [11] His whole approach to the problem of God, his whole message to modern man, was "to make manifest this coherence and to show how solid, natural and total it is." [12]

What Teilhard is attempting to do, then, is to give a basis for believing in the existence of God which could be discussed and established in function of both man's experience of modern life and his experience of Christian faith. The common denominator in each case is human aspiration. "Let us look well," he says, "and we shall find that our faith in God, however isolated it may be, awakens in us a flood of human aspirations. It is in this original source of strength that we must immerse ourselves once more, if we really want to communicate with our brother men." [13] In Teilhard's case such communication necessarily took place in the context of evolution, since he felt this to be the greatest single discovery of modern man about himself. He was convinced that the Christian phenomenon had to be seen within the evolving human phenomenon, and to help people do so, believer and unbeliever alike, he elaborated a dialectic which sought first to show man's need of a transcendent God if evolution is to succeed, and then to show that only faith in Christ can fulfill that need. Let us consider now both poles of what Teilhard calls his "dialectic of spirit."

II

What brought Teilhard as a scientist and a philosopher face to face with the problem of God was the question of a successful outcome for the evolutionary process. His whole psychological preoccupation was, as is well known, with unity and synthesis, and his search for these in his personal life could not but find its counterpart in his life as a scientist. This is the ultimate reason that he searched in scientific data for some law which might allow him to trace the movement of evolution from its beginnings up to the present and thereby situate the human species within the total cosmic phenomenon. The law he elaborated, that of "complexity-consciousness," says that a higher degree of interior consciousness will always correspond in the experimental order to a higher degree of organic complexity. Since in the case of man we have the most complex of organisms, the human brain, we find here as a consequence the highest degree of consciousness, namely the power of reflection. Teilhard did indeed extrapolate this law into the past to explain the origin both of life and of thought, but his primary concern was to know what this law could tell him of the future. In essay after essay, as well as in *The Phenomenon of Man,* he repeats in different contexts and with different emphasis his central argument, and its brief outline here will show how it forces the reader to consider the necessity of an absolute. [14]

For clarity's sake we might divide what he says into three

stages. The first is his insistence that man must be able to see some goal for his activity on earth, that is to say, some terminal point where organically he can develop no further in complexity or, as a consequence, in consciousness. For the movement of cosmogenesis continues in man and becomes a noogenesis in which the human species moves forward by the increasingly complex interplay of that which is specifically human, namely interpersonal relationships on the level of thought, freedom and love. It is precisely the sudden recognition by contemporary man that as a species he is incomplete and that his future development hinges upon his freedom, which has given rise in him to those feelings of anxiety and futility which characterize his life today. "In broad terms it may be affimed that the Human, having become aware of its uncompleted state, cannot lend itself without reluctance, still less give itself with passion, to any course that may attract it unless there be some kind of discernible and definitive consummation to be looked for at the end, if only as a limit. Above all it rejects dispersal and dissolution and the circle from which there is no escape. . . . There must be some peak disclosed at the end of the journey, some transformation capable of giving life. Only such an outlook, only such a hope, is ultimately capable, even under the painful lash of material needs, of sustaining our forward progress to the end." [15]

This conviction of the necessity of man's having some ultimate goal for his action leads Teilhard to a second stage in which he rejects absolutely the possibility that this goal should involve total death. This accounts in fact for his many criticisms of Marxism.[16] "Those who think on Marxist lines," he says, "believe that all that is necessary to polarize the human molecules is that they should look forward to an eventual state of collective reflection and sympathy at the culmination of anthropogenesis, from which all will benefit through participation; a vault of intermingled thoughts, as it were, a closed circuit of attachments in which the individual will achieve intellectual and affective wholeness to the extent that he is at one with the whole system." [17] But such an outlook, Teilhard insists, is simply to work for the mere "well-being" of humanity, whereas what man in his heart really wants is "more-being." This means that he wants to escape death, for ultimate death would mean that the world in which he lived and labored was hermetically closed and that what awaited the human species was the eventual triumph of entropy, pulling humanity back to the subhuman or to nothingness. The vast majority of men are not yet disturbed by this prospect. Today they still imagine, says Teilhard, that they can breathe freely inside an insurmountable barrier of death, provided they can think of it as sufficiently far away. But his own experience and that of many others indicate that tomorrow it will be otherwise. "A kind of panic claustrophobia is going to seize mankind at the mere idea that it could be heremetically sealed up in a closed universe." Why? "Because . . . although reflective existence has always been oriented substantially toward survival forever, there can be no group experience of this primordial polarization until co-reflection around us has reached a certain important critical point." [18]

The "important critical point" in this text refers to that moment when the mass of humanity becomes aware of the importance of love for the unification of mankind. For without love the only alternative for unification is brute force, exterior to man, impersonal, and in opposition to his need freely to choose his own future. But to have love we must suppose that evolution is a movement that does not destroy individual personality but nourishes it. This is why Teilhard insists that the process itself must be irreversible as far as man is concerned, and that death cannot mean the end of the person but must constitute a barrier through which there is passage to a new mode of personal existence. And because love dies in contact with the impersonal and anonymous, "a world culminating in the impersonal can bring us neither the warmth of attraction nor the hope of irreversibility (immortality), and without these individual egotism will always have the last word. What is needed is a real *Ego* at the summit of the world to bring to fulfillment, without confusing them, all the elemental *egos* of earth." Man's faith in the ultrahuman, therefore, his urge toward *some thing* ahead, cannot be fulfilled except by combining with another and still more fundamental aspiration urging him toward *some one.* "Only a genuine 'super-love,' the attractive power of a real 'super-person,' can of psychological necessity dominate, possess and synthesize the host of other earthly loves. Unless such a focus of convergence exists for the universe, not

metaphorical or potential but real, no coherence is possible for
totalized humanity and therefore no true stability." [19]

Let us note carefully at this point some of the implications of
Teilhard's thought at the end of this second stage. Up to now what
he has said is that man will never give himself to the work of
building the earth unless he sees an ultimate goal before him and
unless this goal somehow involves an escape from total death. But
to be convinced of this he must likewise be convinced that the goal
he is striving for must somehow be capable of nourishing personal
love and therefore be itself personal, since love is the highest form
of human energy and is alone capable of motivating truly human
action. Teilhard quite candidly calls this analysis "an act of faith,"
by which he means not a religious act, but an option that the world
in which we live is ultimately intelligible and does not involve
absurdity. An act of faith in this sense, accounting for the totality
of experience, is synonymous, he says, with "an intellectual synthesis" and calls for the intervention of a personal decision.[20]
When such a decision takes place, then we have "the inevitable
intrusion of the problem of God" into science and evolution.[21]
Only by postulating the existence of God can we come to an
understanding of evolution which is coherent, and coherence for
Teilhard is, as we have already noted, the final criterion of truth.
In evolution he saw not simply a scientific hypothesis, but an
experimental affirmation of the coherence of being. By following
out to the end all the implications of such coherence, Teilhard felt
one had to speak of its ultimate source. "Once it is admitted," he
wrote a friend, "that being is better than its opposite, it is difficult
to stop short of God; if it is not admitted, discussion ceases to be
possible." [22]

We are in a position now, I think, better to understand the third
stage of Teilhard's effort to show that the key which unlocks the
meaning of evolution is man's need of an absolute. This third
stage deals with what Teilhard insists must be the attributes of
the God whom man can discover by following out all the implications of the evolutionary process. These attributes appear in
The Phenomenon of Man but some of their presuppositions do not
come through as clearly there as in other texts. There is, first of all,
Teilhard's emphasis upon God as a Person. In 1940 he wrote of the

world war that "the root of the evil is not in the apparent conflicts, but very far from them it seems to me, in the inner fact that men have despaired of God's personality." [23] By this he meant, of course, that man as a person will tend always to fail in love for other men insofar as he does not recognize a divine center for the universe who draws men to himself and to each other precisely as persons, which is to say by love. Unless man accepts a personal God who loves him, all the accumulated potential in the individual, in a given society and in the world at large, will become oriented toward disorder and violence rather than to unification and love. This conviction explains his frequent appeals "that we should overcome the 'anti-personalist' complex which paralyzes us." [24] It also explains his opposition to the pantheism of Eastern thought, which did not distinguish between individual and person and whose ideal of union with God tended to do away with both.[25]

The second attribute of God which Teilhard stresses is his actuality. Here again the center of attention is on the need for the success of evolution of Someone "loving and lovable *at this very moment.*" Love, Teilhard says, "becomes impoverished with remoteness in space—and still more, much more, with difference in time. For love to be possible there must be co-existence. . . . Neither an ideal center nor a potential center could possibly suffice. An actual and real noosphere means an actual and real center." [26] In Teilhard's system, therefore, evolution is not in any sense an autonomous or spontaneous movement of growth in consciousness. It is due not to some mechanical thrust from below but to an attraction from above, "an inverse form of gravitation," as he calls it.[27] This attraction is that exercised by Someone loving upon someone loved, and the more individual men experience the reality of God's love in their lives, the more they themselves will be drawn to him and hence capable of contributing to the growth of spirit. "The spiritual value of a man . . . depends upon the degree of actuality which God has assumed for him; not the degree of speculative or even affective perfection, but, I repeat, the degree of actuality." [28]

Finally there is a third attribute of God which is stressed frequently, namely his transcendence. While it is legitimate to point out that in Teilhard's system the immanence of the divine action in evolution is so emphasized that the *sense* of its transcendence sometimes gets lost, it is nonetheless clear that the *concept* of transcendence is never absent from his thought. Indeed the transcendence of God is quite essential, since an actual personal Center of evolution can in no sense be the product of such evolution. To satisfy the ultimate requirements of our action, says Teilhard, God "must be independent of the collapse of forces with which evolution is woven. . . . While being the last term of [evolution's] series, he is also *outside all series.*" And in another text he says that "in short, God shows himself to us as a *hyper*-center and also inevitably at the same time as an *auto*-center. He is, at least in his most essential self, transcendent, that is to say, independent of evolution, because he exists independent of time and space in that center which is himself." [29] Evolution has, then, what Teilhard calls a "transcendent nucleus," or a "transcendent face," which lies behind that "immanent face" of which we spoke in describing the first stage of his dialectic. This "immanent face" is the terminal point of noogenesis, that collectivity of consciousness which man can discern at the end. What forces man to look behind this fore-seeable summit of the evolutionary cone is the problem of death. For in order to guarantee that man's total development as a person in freedom, consciousness and love will not in the end disappear, there must be a face to evolution which man cannot see, and this must be a Person, actually attracting the human person by love, and bringing the movement of life on earth to a successful close on the other side of the death barrier.

We may bring to a close this treatment of the first pole of Teilhard's dialectic on the problem of God by noting briefly one corollary to this attribute of transcendence, namely our inability directly to experience God's activity in the universe. This follows, first of all, from the fact that the divine action is capable of simultaneously affecting the totality of the universe and all things in it, so that it can at the same time be present everywhere yet not be apprehended by any single individual. Secondly, this same divine action is capable of reaching the deepest part of man, the very center of his being, and of this center of himself man has no direct experience. "Thus," concludes Teilhard, "the precise point touched by the divine power is essentially extra-phenomenal, in the first case because of the degree of its extension, in the second because of the degree of its depth." And then he adds by way of summary: "Properly speaking God does not make things, rather he makes things make themselves." [30] For Teilhard, then, God's activity always takes place under what he calls the phenomenal veil. "For Christian transformism," he writes, "God's creative action is no longer seen as abruptly inserting its work into the midst of pre-existent beings, but rather as *causing to come to birth* in the depths of things the successive terminations of its activity. It is not on this account any less essential, any less universal, nor above all any less intimate to things." [31] Man's experience of God's absence is consequently an experience of his transcendence, and the hiddenness of God, far from being an arbitrary decision not to show himself, is really a manifestation of an otherness which is not too far *outside* to be a phenomenon, but too far *inside*.

III

Thus far we have considered that pole of Teilhard's dialectic on the problem of God which concerns man's need of an absolute. We have not as yet mentioned the word "Omega," but it will be easily seen how Teilhard can apply this term, the last letter of the Greek alphabet, both to the "immanent face" of evolution we have discussed, that goal of collective consciousness which man must see at the end of the process, and also to the "transcendent face," that divine Person responsible for beginning the process and bringing it to completion in himself. Now the second pole of Teilhard's dialectic consists in searching for some confirmation of the existence of such a divine Omega, or more exactly for some indication that this transcendent Center of evolution has himself spoken to man. "A presence is never silent," he once wrote. And in another text he says: "To admit, even by way of conjecture, the existence at the summit of the universe of an Omega Point, is *ipso facto* to introduce the possibility that some influences, some radiations of a psychic nature, circulate around us, betraying and at the same time confirming . . . the postulated existence beyond ourselves of an ultra-cosmic pole of personal energy. And it is here precisely that we see clearly the meaning and importance of the Christian phenomenon." [32] The second pole of Teilhard's dialectic will deal, then, with that need of modern man which Teilhard sees as a concretization of his need of an absolute, namely his need of Christ.

What Teilhard seeks to do first is to show the remarkable correspondence between the cosmic function of Omega, postulated by his analysis of evolution, and what Christian revelation tells us of the cosmic role of Christ. Thus what he stresses primarily from this point of view is that relationship of Christ to the cosmos which appears so clearly in St. Paul, St. John and in Greek patristic thought. Through this optic the Incarnation becomes the visible manifestation of the union of God with mankind and the material world. This is why Teilhard speaks so often of the "universal Christ" and the "cosmic Christ." Here again, as in his earlier approach to the need of Omega through the problem of death, he is grappling with a problem which is his own: "Were the exigencies of my personal religion," he asked, "so exceptional and so new that no traditional formula could satisfy them?" Such a formula, however, was at hand in traditional Christian teaching, although it had not been in the forefront of the Christian conscience for many centuries. When Teilhard discovered it he gave it his own distinctive interpretation: "The universal Christ, such as I personally understand him, is a synthesis of Christ and the universe. Not a new divinity, but rather the inevitable interpretation of the mystery which is the summation of Christianity: the Incarnation." [33] This outlook is developed at some length in the Epilogue to *The Phenomenon of Man,* and it will be worth citing the key text at length:

As early as in St. Paul and St. John we read that to create, to fulfill and to purify the world is, for God, to unify it by uniting it organically to himself. How does he unify it? By partially immersing himself in things, by becoming an 'element,' and then, from this vantage point at the heart of matter, assuming the control and leadership of what we now call evolution. Christ, the universal principle of vitalization because born as a man among men, put himself in a position (maintained ever since) to subdue, to purify, to direct, and to superanimate the general ascent of consciousnesses into which he inserted himself. By a perennial act of communion and sublimation, he aggregates to himself the total psychism of the earth. And when he has gathered everything together and transformed everything, he will close in upon himself and his conquests, thereby rejoining, in a final gesture, the divine focus he has never really left. Then as St. Paul tells us, *God shall be all in all.* This is indeed a superior form of 'pantheism' without trace of the poison of adulteration or annihilation: the expectation of perfect unity, steeped in which each element will reach its consummation at the same time as the universe. The universe fulfilling itself in a synthesis of centers in perfect conformity with the laws of union. God, the Center of centers. In that final vision Christian dogma finds its culmination.[34]

Having underlined the correspondence between the *cosmic* function of Christ, as developed in one area of Christian theology, and the cosmic function of Omega, as developed in his own system of thought, Teilhard goes on to underline the *personal* role of Christ and the significance of the Christian doctrine of love within an evolutionary world view. In such a world view, it will be remembered, love is the key to survival. For evolution to succeed, there must be growth of a universal love in the noosphere. But where in man's present experience can we find the beginnings of such a love? Nowhere, Teilhard insists, more than in the life of the contemporary Christian for whom creation has become meaningful in terms of evolution and for whom Christ is the source of love. "Such a believer sees the history of the world as a vast movement of cosmogenesis, in the course of which all the varied fibers of reality converge, without losing their identity, in a Christ at once personal and cosmic. The Christian who understands both what is essential to his faith and what is the spatiotemporal interrelatedness of nature, finds himself (I am speaking realistically not metaphorically) in the marvelous position of being able, in the midst of the most varied activities and in union with the whole of mankind, to achieve a unique experience of communion. . . . Thus we see that Christ (provided he is disclosed in the full realism of his Incarnation) is in every way comparable to the Omega Point which our theory made us anticipate, for he tends to produce exactly the spiritual totalization which we await." [35]

These two roles of Christ in traditional Christian teaching, the one cosmic, the other personal, the one seeing him as Lord of all things created and source of their stability, the other as the channel of God's love and the source of its presence among men, were responsible for what Teilhard calls "an ultimate and final definition of the Omega Point." Omega is the Person of Christ who, through his Incarnation within history and his Parousia at its end, acts as a unifying focus for three centers, one inside the other, which reach a point at the top of the cone of time. The outside center is the natural summit of the humano-cosmic cone; within this is the supernatural summit of the humano-Christic cone; and the innermost center is the transcendent Being who through Christ has made himself also immanent.[36] Teilhard was convinced, moreover, that the Omega postulated by reason and the Omega acknowledged through Christian faith would eventually react upon each other in the consciousness of mankind, and in the end be synthesized together. He saw the cosmic in this way giving greater significance to the Christic, and the Christic in turn "amorizing" the whole of the cosmic. "A truly inevitable and 'implosive' encounter, this, and its probable effect will be soon after to weld together . . . the scientific and the spiritual around a Christ identified at last, two thousand years after the confession of Peter . . . as the ultimate summit and the only God possible for an evolutionary movement finally recognized as convergent. This is what I see ahead and it is this for which I am waiting." [37]

What Teilhard is ultimately suggesting, then, in his whole approach to the contemporary problem of God, is that modern man try to look upon the world and to see what he sees. This means, first of all, seeing man's existence within the new perspective of evolutionary change, a perspective demanding faith in survival after death as well as in a divine center of unification who must make this survival possible. But to share his vision means also to see a correspondence between this "faith in the world," as he often calls it, and another faith, not a result of rational analysis but a response to Christian revelation. This faith in the Person and cosmic role of Jesus of Nazareth completed Teilhard's faith in the world, and gave him a certainty of an outcome for evolution which his own extrapolations into the future could not give. "From the moment that we admit the reality of an answer coming from above," he writes, "we move somehow into the order of certainty. But this takes place not by reason of a simple confrontation of subject and object, but from contact between two centers of consciousness: an act not so much of knowledge as of recognition, the whole complex interplay of two beings who freely open and give themselves to each other." [38]

At the beginning of this chapter we noted Teilhard's realization that his own experience of God, both as a man and as a Christian, had to be conceptualized in the context of modern man's determination to dedicate himself to human progress and to become master of the world in which he lives. He was likewise painfully aware that the vast majority of believers were not trying to do this at all, and that as a result their belief in God would eventually become irrelevant, if not for themselves at least for their children. "There is only one way for believers to bring God to the men of our time," he insisted, "and that is to share their human ideal, and to search at their side for the God whom we already possess but who is present among us yet as if we did not recognize him." [39] This "presence" of God to modern man, a presence experienced more often than not as an absence, is for Teilhard a presence manifested in and through the events of man's life in the world. Only such an understanding of God, he felt, was capable of bridging the growing chasm between Christian faith and contemporary culture. His Christology was a further effort in this same direction: faith in the Incarnation is precisely a recognition that God has become so immanent in human life that the distinction between sacred and secular must henceforth be considered more rational than real. The Christian experience is simply that of taking part in God's plan, and this plan embraces the whole of the universe, the secular and the sacred, everything which is the work of man, everything which is the work of God. "And thus in the end," concludes Teilhard, "above the rediscovered greatness of man, above the newly revealed greatness of humanity, not violating but preserving the integrity of science, the face of God reappears in our modern world." [40]

VIII

Change and Balance in Christian Life

There is to be found in the churches at present a growing awareness, especially among the young, of the inadequacy of a large segment of what has generally been called Christian spirituality. I am not speaking here of practical matters, such as the amount of time given to private prayer, the mode of conducting liturgical worship, the value of this or that rule or formula, or even the emphasis today upon individual freedom and initiative. Since the Second Vatican Council the Roman Catholic Church as a whole has been moving away from an insistence upon conformity, and it is therefore normal that we should find all around us a search for new ideas and a willingness to experiment with new modes of spiritual formation. The problem, however, is the framework within which such experimentation takes place, the mental outlook, the "view" as Newman would call it, which is the ultimate factor in anyone's style of approach to God. Over the centuries modifications in Christian living have more or less taken place within a certain fixed framework of thought, and it is precisely this fundamental Christian image of life which is now undergoing reappraisal. This is no easy matter. It is one thing to reject old styles and attitudes and quite another to get along without them or put new ones in their place. The danger, moreover, is that the new image we create may filter out completely certain balancing elements in the old image, so that our new view of life may produce in the end just as many difficulties, psychological and spiritual, as our old.

Now without doubt the most symbolic figure in the formation of this new Christian image of the world is Pierre Teilhard de Chardin. Christians generally feel that he has given voice to much of what they experience but find difficult to articulate. "The great converters (or perverters) of man," wrote Teilhard, "have always been those who have burned most intensely with the spirit of their times." [1] What Teilhard has done is to articulate a set of positive emphases in spirituality which the modern Christian spontaneously embraces. These range over three large areas in human living, and I would like to consider each of them briefly in the pages which follow. Not only are they viable for the twentieth century, but they emerge from its very core, and they are eloquent testimony that in its interaction with the world the Christian intelligence is fundamentally creative. Yet what I wish to stress also is that, in articulating this set of emphases which are instinctively accepted by the modern Christian, Teilhard also provides a set of balances. It is these balancing affirmations which are especially necessary today lest the spirituality we are in process of developing go to extremes, and lose thereby its distinctively Christian character. The theme of this study, then, is that the spirituality found in the writings of Teilhard de Chardin is thoroughly modern and at the same time authentically Christian.

I

The first positive emphasis emerging in modern Christian spirituality concerns the importance of the material world in man's relationship to God. The traditional dichotomies between natural-supernatural, body-spirit, divine-human, immanent-transcendent, sacred-secular, are becoming more and more irrelevant for the modern Christian. This is not to say that he does not recognize a distinction between what is represented by these terms when such distinctions are explained to him. The point is rather that these distinctions no longer have any significance in his spiritual development. He wants to be more deeply Christian, but he resents being told that he must therefore become less secular, because deep down he suspects that anyone today less concerned for the secular is liable also to be less Christian. Nor can such an outlook be labeled an innovation, a reversal of Christian tradition. More than one theologian has pointed out that this attitude is in fact a renewal of the early Judeo-Christian sense of man's unity with matter and his relationship to God through matter. No biblical writer could ever conceive man without his body, nor could he ever disassociate man's body from God's salvific action. The "angelism" which crept into Christian spirituality toward the end of the patristic era came not from Sacred Scripture but from Augustine and Pseudo-Dionysius; and its source in both cases seems to have been the thought of Plotinus, who according to Porphyry "seemed ashamed of being in the body." [2]

The thought of Teilhard de Chardin has given a strong impetus to this concern for the material world in one's relationship to God. Indeed, his whole evolutionary system puts such strong emphasis on the continuity of matter and spirit that he has been accused by philosophers of being a materialist and by scientists of ignoring the concrete in order to speculate about what cannot be experimentally verified. In his theological speculation, he insisted again and again that theologians give serious consideration to the physical relationship between Christ and the material world. For it is precisely the physical mediation of Christ's Body-Person, he said, which gives impetus to the evolution itself, makes ultimate sense out of man's effort to build the earth, and is finally destined to bring the material world to its consummation in God-Omega. "The whole of the Church's dogmatic and sacramental economy," he wrote, "teaches us to respect matter and to value it. Christ had to assume and wanted to assume real flesh. He sanctifies human flesh by special contact and he prepares its physical resurrection. . . . Because it has been assimilated into the Body of Christ, something from matter is destined to pass into the foundations and walls of the heavenly Jerusalem." [3] The rise of "technopolis," therefore, far from being a reason for pessimistic concern, is in reality an occasion for the Christian to devote himself more completely to the world and thereby to realize in himself the full meaning of the Incarnation.

When Teilhard applied this theological speculation to Christian living, what resulted was a call to experience God in the secular world in a way that was impossible for Christians of a former age. He once complained that manuals of ascetical theology usually accepted as axiomatic that growth in spirit could only come by separating what was assumed to be the two basic components of the universe, the pure and the impure.[4] This he rejected as Manichaean. It injects one's spiritual life, he said, with a dualism which allows only partial commitment to the world, forcing the Christian in the end to lead a double life, so that he belongs neither wholly to God nor wholly to things. What was needed, he urged, was for spiritual writers to concern themselves with the material world, "to discover what there could be that is divine and predestined within the matter itself of our cosmos, our humanity and our progress." [5] The supernatural is a ferment, he wrote in another essay, not a finished organism. Its role is to transform nature, but it cannot do so apart from the matter which nature provides it with.[6]

Now as we shall see in a moment, Teilhard was well aware that such stress on the importance of the material world in one's relationship to God is not without its dangers. Not everyone today who writes on this subject, however, would seem to have such an awareness. In *The Secular City*, Harvey Cox says that the Gospel is "a call to imaginative urbanity and mature secularity," and nothing more.[7] There is no concern at all in his book for any direct personal relationship between God and man. "Like his relationship to his work partner, man's relationship to God derives from the work they do together. . . . God manifests himself to us in and through secular events." [8] This is true enough, but such an "I-You" relationship, as Cox calls it, can scarcely have any Christian significance unless it is based upon a prior "I-Thou" relationship, a direct turning toward God present in the human heart. God indeed manifests himself in the material world and in the events of our lives, but we shall never find him there unless we have first found him within ourselves. Significantly enough, there is no mention of prayer in *The Secular City*, no mention of converse of any kind either with Christ or with the Father. Rather the impression is conveyed that any such I-Thou relationship would be inimical to one's involvement in the human task. "God wants man to be interested not in him but in his fellow man," says Cox.[9]

Teilhard, on the other hand, was not at all content with the abstract statement that God manifests himself to us in and through the material world. What he wanted was actually to find God, to be aware of his presence in people and things, to possess him and be possessed by him. "The veneer of color and scene bores me to tears," he once wrote from China. "What I love is hidden. . . . Even when I am most absorbed in geology, my interest has already wandered elsewhere. It is the Other that I seek." [10] Such an attitude toward matter explains why Teilhard could look upon the world as a crystal lamp illumined from within by the light of Christ.[11] This image, mentioned first in a 1916 essay, is a graphic illustration of the idea which will impregnate all his writings, even the most philosophical and scientific, namely that there is a creative presence of Christ in everyone and everything everywhere, a universal and cosmic "diaphany," as he calls it, which began with his historical epiphany. This presence is therefore a human as well as a divine presence, founded upon the physical relationship of Christ's Body-Person through whom the creative action of God is channeled.

> Like those translucent materials which can be wholly illumined by a light enclosed within them, the world manifests itself to the Christian mystic as bathed in an inward light. . . . This light . . . is the tranquil, mighty radiance born of the synthesis in Jesus of all the elements of the world. The more completely the beings thus illumined attain their natural fulfillment, the closer and more perceptible this radiance will be.[12]

Or consider the following text:

> Lord, God, grant that the light of your countenance may shine forth for me in other men. . . . Grant me to see you . . . above all in the most inward, most perfect, most remote levels of the souls of my brothers. The gift you ask of me for these brothers of mine . . . is not the overflowing tenderness of those special, preferential loves which you implant in our lives, but something less tender, though just as real and even more strong. Your will is that, with the help of

your Eucharist, there should be revealed between me and my brother-men that basic attraction . . . which mystically transforms the myriads of rational creatures into a single monad, as it were, in you, Christ Jesus.[13]

This overreaching desire of Teilhard to see through the world of people and things and find God is the reason why he is at such pains to show that material evolution is ultimately oriented toward growth of the spiritual. Thus the function he assigns to his law of complexity-consciousness is that of allowing the "within" of things to emerge, to promote growth in "consciousness," by the interplay of radial and tangential energy. Unlike many physical scientists, Teilhard refused to see in the law of entropy a gloomy prediction that the universe will one day run down completely and stop. Such a law, he felt, told us only about the "without" of things and left untouched the world of spirit "within." "The whole movement of material growth in the universe," he wrote, "is ultimately directed toward spirit, and the whole movement of spiritual growth is ultimately directed toward Christ." [14] Hence he could pray: "By virtue of your suffering Incarnation, disclose to us the spiritual power of matter, and then teach us to harness it jealously for you." [15]

Gabriel Vahanian has written that there is no reason why secularity, by which he means involvement in the world for the sake of God's glory, should ever slip into secularism, or what he calls an immanentist religiosity.[16] This may indeed be true, but only if the person involved is ultimately seeking to possess God through this involvement. He will find God in people and things only if he wants to find him there. This is why Teilhard, while rejecting a spirituality based exclusively upon the pure intention, puts such emphasis himself upon the virtue of purity in his own spirituality. This he defines, interestingly enough, as "the rectitude and impulse introduced into our lives by the love of God sought in and above everything." The intensity of this purity in men increases and is measured by the "degree of attraction that draws them to the divine Center." The sanctification of human effort depends, then, he continues, "upon the initial and fundamental role of one's intention, which is indeed . . . the golden key which unlocks our interior world to the presence of God. . . . It is God and God alone whom [the Christian] pursues through the reality of created things. His interest lies truly in things but in absolute dependence upon God's presence in them." [17]

These texts of Teilhard are sufficient, I think, to underline the point I am making. Christian spirituality is undergoing a long overdue change of style, and one of the elements in this change is the growing emphasis upon the importance of the material world. Teilhard has encouraged this emphasis, has to some degree even been responsible for it, insofar as he insists upon the relationship of Christ to the universe and the consequent significance of human work as a cooperation in the creative action of God. Yet this thoroughly modern emphasis has a tendency to overlook what Teilhard never overlooked, namely that building the earth can have no Christian significance except insofar as individual men give it that significance; and this they do by their union with Christ and their desire above all else to seek and to find him in every earthly task to which they commit themselves. Only then will they have a right to say with Teilhard that nothing here below is profane for those who know how to see.[18] For such "seeing" is a gift of God and is given only to those who desire it. This is the first of the balances which Teilhard brings to his spirituality of human conquest, and it keeps this spirituality authentically Christian. We might summarize it in a final text in which Teilhard speaks once more of purity:

> To be pure of heart means to love God above all things and at the same time to see him everywhere in all things. Whether the just man is rising above and beyond all creatures to an almost immediate awareness of Godhead or throwing himself upon the world to conquer it and bring it to perfection, as it is every man's duty to do, he will have eyes only for God. . . . The pure heart is the heart which, surmounting the multiple and disruptive pull of created things, fortifies its unity, that is to say, matures its spirituality, in the fire of the divine simplicity.[19]

II

There is a second emphasis emerging strongly today in Christian spirituality. This is the emphasis upon self-fulfillment in man's relationship with God. Here again, what we are experiencing is a reaction against a certain anti-humanist tendency in spiritual teaching. Frequently the test of one's union with God was one's willingness to embrace an ideal that was very often in opposition to one's development as a man. Hence the importance placed on certain ascetical practices, the performance of fixed penances, and the overall suspicion of any purely spontaneous natural inclination. The rigidity of obedience was a natural offshoot of this: the spiritual ideal was never to do one's own will, always the will of another. Other things being equal, the work one was engaged in was presumed to have more value insofar as one did not really enjoy it. Many of the agonizing problems of conscience today in regard to sexual morality have their ultimate roots in the belief that even though sex was not evil in itself, it could hardly be more than tolerated in someone aspiring to lead a full Christian life. The emphasis upon the deleterious effects of original sin, upon the passion and death of Christ rather than upon his resurrection and glory, upon the sacrificial aspects of charity rather than upon the joy of community living, upon resignation in defeat rather than battle for victory, all this set a style to Christian spirituality against which there are now open resentment and rejection.

This should come as no surprise to anyone. We are living in the era of the person. The value of the human person in all his uniqueness and freedom is perhaps the single most influential discovery of modern man. From it has come the new stress on personal initiative, responsibility and freedom. Christian spirituality must offer fulfillment to the person, and it must offer it to him now, not in some future life with which the present life has seemingly little connection. The ideal which the modern Christian wants is the ideal of the fully human. Far from being a desire to have things easy, such an ideal in fact inspires the greatest generosity, and involves a readiness to endure almost any inconvenience and hardship to help the underprivileged and to further the great social movements of our day. Witness the present response to the civil rights movement and to the call of the Peace Corps. Witness the uncompromising intellectual honesty of young people, their repudiation of violence and hypocrisy, their desire to be close to others in community. Such an outlook, moreover, has been strongly seconded by the Second Vatican Council in its Pastoral Constitution on the Church in the Modern World. Its emphasis upon the humanizing influence of Christ is a clear departure in tone for ecclesial documents. Christ is he who "fully reveals man to man himself" and "whoever follows after Christ, the perfect man, becomes himself more of a man." For it is Christ who "animates, purifies, and strengthens those noble longings too by which the human family strives to make its life more human and to render the whole earth submissive to this goal." Indeed, it is precisely the plan of God that the Church "contribute greatly toward making the family of man and its history more human." [20]

This relationship between Christianity and self-fulfillment worried Teilhard all his life. "How is one to be more fully a Christian than anyone," he asked early in life, "and at the same time more fully a man?" For what he feared was precisely that he might "remain uncommitted among my fellow men, and because of my religion they will regard me as a deserter who is only half a man. . . . It is absolutely necessary that Christ be as large as my life, my whole life. I must have an awareness of growing in him, not only by asceticism and the painful wrench of suffering . . . but also by whatever positive effort I am capable of, whatever is naturally perfective in my human achievement. I must have this awareness, I say, otherwise Christianity would be robbing me of the courage to act." [21] At another time he asked, "To be a Christian must I really give up trying to be human, human in the widest and deepest sense of the word, totally and passionately human?" [22] Five years before his death he admits that all during his life he had been "compelled by an inner constraint to leave the well-beaten track of a certain traditional type of asceticism not fully human, in order to search out a way to heaven along which the whole dynamism of matter and flesh can pass by way of synthesis into the birth of spirit. . . . To reach heaven by bringing earth to perfection. To Christify matter. That is the whole adventure of my life, a great and magnificent adventure, during which I am still often afraid, but to which it was impossible not to have committed myself." [23]

This last text implies what Teilhard said explicitly more than once, namely that certain risks are involved in leaving "the beaten track of a certain traditional type of asceticism not fully human." Hence his concern to integrate into his ideal of the fully human a set of balances. These he summarized briefly in a 1943 essay on human happiness: "To be fully human and fully alive, a man must first be centered on himself, then centered away from himself in others, and finally centered beyond himself in Someone greater than he." [24] It is possible today, by emphasizing self-fulfillment, to lose sight of the corresponding need in our relationship with God of the second two experiences which Teilhard stresses here, namely that of decentering or detachment, and that of purification or what he calls a "surcentering" upon God. He believed, first of all, that any man truly devoted to the human, though outwardly he might be immersed in the concerns of earth, must become a man of great detachment. Detachment for him is in fact inseparable from true possession. "To create or organize material energy, or truth, or beauty, brings with it inner torment which prevents those who face its hazards from sinking into the quiet and closed-in life wherein grows the vice of self-regard and attachment. . . . Over and over again he must go beyond himself, tear himself away from himself, leaving behind him his most cherished beginnings." [25] Especially is this true of the Christian, for he knows that his function is to divinize the world in Jesus Christ, and consequently in him that detachment through action should reach its maximum.

The Christian, who is by right the first and most human of men, is more subject than others to the psychological reversal whereby, in the case of intelligent creatures, joy in action imperceptibly melts into desire for submission, and the exaltation of becoming one's own self into the zeal to die in another. Having been perhaps primarily alive to the attractions of union with God through action, he begins to conceive and then to desire a complementary aspect, an ulterior phase, in his communion: one in which he would not develop himself so much as lose himself in God.[26]

This mention of losing oneself in God brings us to the second balance never far from Teilhard's mind, and also indicates how closely the two balances are linked together. For in every Christian life, detachment must lead to purification and there is no purification without pain. This is why there is in Teilhard a constant awareness of the harsh realities of life, above all the reality of death. The experience of death was in fact a primordial experience for him, and its theme appears again and again in his writings.[27] For this experience of human self-fulfillment cut short and of hopes shattered is one that no man can avoid. What is the use of an emphasis on self-fulfillment if it can all be swept aside in a moment by death or by war, or by the greed and stupidity of man? And how is self-fulfillment to be integrated into the feelings of futility which come with sickness, human misunderstandings, or the inevitable failures which must somehow be part of every effort to take part in the creative activity of God? Teilhard would be quite disturbed were he to hear what is not infrequently said today, that modern man looks upon life as a set of problems, not an unfathomable mystery, that he consequently spends little time thinking about the so-called ultimate questions. Teilhard's reaction might well be that whoever this modern man is, he is not Christian man. For the real world for the Christian is the world where Christ was crucified, and if the cross means anything it must mean that all men, even those who labor to improve the world and fulfill themselves as men, must expect and accept suffering before achievement, self-renunciation before self-fulfillment, and death before true life.

It is very significant that a man so committed to human fulfillment could write to a close friend in 1934: "What we have to learn is to preserve a real appetite for life and action while at the same time renouncing once and for all any desire to be happy just for ourselves. There is the secret—and not the illusion—of living in the divine Milieu." [28] He meant this too, for he wrote to another friend that we must "cherish, along with the fulfillments in our life, everything that diminishes us, that is to say, all the passive purifications which Christ has planned for us in order to transform into himself those elements of our personality which we seek to develop for him." [29] It is perfectly true that Teilhard was most concerned with the positive meaning of the cross, the support given by Christ's sufferings and death to the pain of human endeavor and to the upward movement of man in the noosphere. Yet he has put no less emphasis than St. John of the Cross upon those passive purifications in the spiritual life which, as far as we can see, do nothing at all for our human endeavor. In these cases, he says, human wisdom is altogether out of its depth. "At every moment we see diminishments, both in us and around us, which do not seem to be compensated by advantages on any perceptible plane, premature deaths, stupid accidents, weaknesses affecting the highest reaches of our being. Under blows such as these man does not move upward in any direction that we can perceive; he disappears or remains grievously diminished." [30] How then, he asks, can such diminishments, which are altogether without compensation, wherein we see death at its most deathly, become for us a good?

His answer is that of John of the Cross: faith. "As a result of [God's] omnipotence impinging on our faith, events which show themselves experimentally in our lives as pure loss will become an immediate factor in the union we dream of establishing with him. Uniting oneself means, in every case, migrating, and dying partially to what one loves. . . . We can therefore set no limits to the tearing up of roots that is involved in our journey to God. . . . God must in some way or other make room for himself, hollowing us out and emptying us, if he is finally to penetrate into us. And in order to assimilate us to him, he must break the molecules of our being so as to re-cast and re-model us. . . . And the more threatening and irreducible reality appears, the more firmly and desperately we must believe." [31] This emphasis upon the role of pure diminishment in the spiritual life, and upon the corresponding need of faith to support such diminishment, is, I submit, an important balance which must be inserted into the modern Christian emphasis on self-fulfillment. For the danger is precisely that when such self-fulfillment is halted, or diminished or even destroyed, we shall not have the resources to react as we must in faith, if the plan of God for our lives is to be accomplished. "We believers," wrote Teilhard, "have the strength and glory of having a faith in God more profound than our faith in the world; and that faith in God re-emerges and persists even when our faith in the world should be crushed by the impact of events." [32] There is need to remind ourselves of this today, for it will insure that our instinctive desire for self-fulfillment in our relations with God and our fellow men will remain an authentically Christian desire, purified in the end of selfishness and pride.

III

There is a third emphasis which characterizes the Christian's relationship with God today, and it may be described quite simply as relativism. Its origin is the thoroughly modern experience of rapid change at all levels of human life. An ever-growing sense of history has removed the cloak of stability which institutions of all types, as well as procedures and modes of thought, have inevitably sought to throw around themselves. Whatever is labeled "traditional" is by this very fact subject to suspicion and loss of confidence, unless the needs of the present and especially the experience of the present can be appealed to for its support. On the cognitive level the problem is whether one can be absolutely certain about anything anymore. Hence the extreme difficulty of total commitment to any one tradition, doctrine or way of life. In a world where pluralism is widespread in religion, philosophy and general human culture, it is no longer an easy thing to accept the Church as something unique, her pronouncements as more than directives, her authority in matters other than revelation as more than provisional. In the area of spirituality this means that the Church is looked upon more as a society in process than as a finished community, and that universal and fixed patterns are no longer seen as essential to one's spiritual life.

Although it is seldom adverted to, the relativism we have just described has a fairly broad and generally positive psychological base. This is the contemporary orientation toward the future.

In a brilliant essay a number of years ago, Robert Johann put his finger on the nerve center of this all-pervading expectancy of modern man, who sees the fragments of the present chiefly as building blocks for tomorrow. Such an outlook leaves room for very few absolutes, and one's life as a consequence becomes crowded with relatives. Each succeeding day becomes merely a springboard to the next, a foothold in reality where one cannot rest, and from which one must constantly project himself into what has not yet come to be. Such an orientation is capable of engendering great enthusiasm for the work at hand, a desire to build a world that will be better both for oneself and for the community. On the negative side, however, the danger is frequently enough dissatisfaction and restlessness, tension and anxiety. The "now" of one's life becomes a mere point of transition, a dot on the horizontal line of becoming, a scene glimpsed from the window of a rushing train whose only meaning is to mark the stages of one's journey. The tendency then is a readiness to work without tranquility and to hope without possession. Since the peace and happiness one craves are in such cases forever eluding one's grasp, "progress" inevitably becomes a wheel to which one is chained, inexorably moving forward yet never coming to rest.[33]

There is no need to elaborate here on the impetus which Teilhard's evolutionary system has given to this orientation of modern man toward the future. "The world holds no interest for me unless I look forward," he told a good friend, "but when my eyes are on the future it is full of excitement."[34] And again: "The past has revealed to me how the future is built, and preoccupation with the future tends to sweep everything else aside."[35] Hope, he wrote in a 1941 essay on progress, must spring to life spontaneously in every generous spirit faced with the task that awaits us. Hope for the future is that which enables us to work in the present. "It is the essential *impulse* without which nothing can be done. A passionate longing to grow, to be, is what we need. . . . Life is ceaseless discovery. Life is movement."[36] Nor did Teilhard hesitate to rebuke the Christians he knew for failing to integrate their human hope in man into their supernatural hope in God, for in Teilhard's system the object of the world's development as well as the source of this development is the Person of Christ. "O you of little faith, why fear or hold aloof from the onward march of the world? Why foolishly multiply your prophecies of woe. On the contrary, we must try everything for Christ; we must hope everything for Christ. *Nihil intentatum,* that is the true Christian attitude. . . . We can never know all that the Incarnation still asks of the world's potentialities. We can never hope for too much from the growing unity of mankind." [37] In the epilogue to *The Divine Milieu* he again reproaches the Christian for his unconcern in uniting his hope in Christ with his hope in man, for his failure to do so is in large measure responsible for the fact that the world's expectation is today no longer Christian. The well-known passage is worth citing at length:

> Expectation—anxious, collective and operative expectation of an end of the world, that is to say of an outcome for the world—that is perhaps the supreme Christian function and the most distinctive characteristic of our religion. . . . The Israelites were constantly expectant, and the first Christians too. . . . Successors to Israel we Christians have been charged with keeping the flame of desire ever alive in the world. Only twenty centuries have passed since the ascension. What have we made of our expectancy? . . . How many of us are genuinely moved in the depths of our hearts by the wild hope that our earth will be recast? . . . Where is the Catholic as passionately vowed (by conviction and not by convention) to spreading the hopes of the Incarnation as many humanitarians are to spreading the dream of the new city? We persist in saying that we keep vigil in expectation of the Master. But in reality we should have to admit, if we were sincere, that we no longer expect anything.[38]

Nevertheless, there is risk in stressing this element of dynamic change in all human life and institutions, and it comes from not anchoring such change in the changeless. The risk is especially great today, for in religious circles we are in full reaction against what can only be called an enthusiasm to absolutize the relative. This has produced the inevitable predisposition not to recognize any absolutes at all. Teilhard himself did not have this problem. His psychological need for some absolute was itself something of an absolute for him. "As far back as I go into my childhood, nothing appears to me more characteristic or familiar in my interior make-up than the taste or irresistible need for something all sufficient and all necessary. To be really satisfied and completely happy meant for me knowing that something 'essential' exists, of which all else is merely addition and ornament." [39] His evolutionary system was an extension of this psychological need, an effort to endow cosmogenesis with a stability it could not otherwise have had, by demanding for its very existence a real attraction from a real, supreme, personal Being. In order to understand the dynamism of the process itself, we are thus forced to recognize the primacy of being over becoming and of act over potency. His absolute was thus outside the process, present both at its beginning and at its end, and it provided that assurance of ultimate success which was alone capable of assuaging the anxiety of modern man.

Yet Teilhard was not unaware of the risk we have mentioned insofar as it manifests itself on the psychological level. For man has to feel that the present is more than a moment in a process; though essentially changing it must somehow transcend change. Hence Teilhard's insistence upon a balance, namely the dimension given to human hopes and aspirations by Christian charity. It is not necessary at this point to recall the decisive role played by love energy in his system of thought. This analysis has been made elsewhere.[40] It is sufficient here simply to underline once more Teilhard's conviction that love changes everything in a man's outlook on life. The central deficiency in all naturalistic humanisms is, he felt, that they ignore the power of love, and this is why the enthusiasm and zeal they engender eventually dry up and become cold, joyless and hard. For a Christian, on the other hand,

> . . . the real is charged with a divine presence in the entirety of its tangible layers. As the mystics knew and felt, everything becomes physically and literally lovable in God; and, conversely, God can be possessed and loved in everything around us. . . . What can this mean except that every action, as soon as it is oriented towards him, takes on, without any change in itself, the psychic character of a center to center relationship, that is to say, of an act of love.[41]

Through charity, then, man can unite himself to the terminus of all human progress, even while dedicating himself to the onward movement at any particular moment in time. The union accomplished in loving and being loved by God transcends the whole order of becoming, and thereby balances expectation with possession, and surrounds the relative with an all-embracing absolute. This is why the creative presence of God in the world is so central a theme in Teilhard's thought. He sees the whole movement of evolution as a mode by which the divine presence is mediated to the world, and it is precisely by charity that we enter into this presence. To the extent that one's commitment to an endless series of relatives is impregnated with charity, it becomes an element in one's union with God and therefore of absolute significance. It becomes a force for promoting the peace and capacity to rest which so many have lost in the turmoil of our technological age.

Teilhard, however, was not content simply to emphasize the importance of charity as a balance to the danger of relativism. He was much more concerned with locating its source. This he found through what may well be one of his most original contributions to theology, namely his insight into the Church as a phylum of love inserted by God into the evolutionary process to guarantee that the human phylum reach the fullness of its natural and supernatural development. The individual Christian's daily life is therefore related to an absolute not simply because it is motivated subjectively by charity, but much more so because it takes place within an objective, corporate, and highly organized phylum, whose function in God's plan is to act as the source of love energy in the world.[42]

This concept is of no small importance today. For alongside the relativism in the modern Christian's outlook, there is likewise a keen and ever-growing awareness that community based on love is absolutely essential to human life, and a fortiori to Christian life. The problem is that for many today traditional forms of Christian life and even religious life do not sufficiently mediate charity as a felt experience. This is not the time to discuss the reasons for this. The point I wish to make is that Teilhard had this same experience long before most of today's Christians were born. For my own part, I hope never to have to go through what he went through in his dealings with religious and ecclesiastical authority.[43] Yet however hemmed in he was by the authoritarianism of his day, his reverence and respect for authority remained profound. The reason was precisely his need of an absolute. "Only in the Roman 'trunk'," he wrote as late as 1950, "do I see the biological support sufficiently vast and differentiated to carry out the enduring transformation of humanity which we await."[44] What Teilhard is telling us, perhaps, is that every man has need not only to possess an absolute among all the relatives of his life, but that he has need also to incarnate that absolute, to locate it. In other words there has to be an objective absolute for every man as well as a subjective absolute. The Catholic Church was this for Teilhard, not in her mere external organization or her changing attitudes, not in her human aspects, therefore, but in that which is divine. St. Paul called the Church Christ's Body, the Bride of Christ; the Fathers called her *Mater Ecclesia*. Teilhard was grasping for the same reality when he spoke of her as the phylum of love. It would not be out of place for the modern Christian to ask what she means to him. We live during one of those times in history when it is imperative that all her defects be clearly evident to the world as well as the contingency of much of what she says and does. But she does contain within herself an absolute, and it is this absolute which we are in desperate need of today to balance our equally desperate need to emphasize the relative in our spiritual life.

IV

The theme of this study has been that the thought of Teilhard de Chardin supports to the full what is most characteristic today in Christian spirituality, namely the emphases upon the material, the personal and the relative. His instinctive spiritual sense, however, has enabled him to maintain as balances the three corresponding emphases upon finding God in the material, integrating the cross into personal development, and impregnating the relatives of human life with love. It is these emphases and these

balances which make his own spirituality both thoroughly modern
and authentically Christian. We might note, moreover, before
we close, the growing importance of Teilhard's overriding concern for what he calls quite simply "the world." This constitutes,
I think, his single most significant contribution to modern Christian spirituality. For since spirituality in its broadest sense is a
style of approach to God, an attitude toward life, each era must
have its own, with its own set of images and its own motivations
corresponding to the Christian needs of a given time. Thus, in
the apostolic era it was the Parousia which fired the Christian
imagination; in a later era the blood of the martyrs; still later
the quarrels between Protestant and Catholic; and in recent centuries the intense missionary activity of Christians. Today what
motivates people is "the world." Christians want to feel they can
reach God through the world, through the whole scientific, technological, humanistic enterprise. But not until Teilhard appeared
on the scene has anyone succeeded in showing them how. He is
the only one who has given this vivid image of modern man a
completely Christian explanation.

"For a long time," he once wrote, "my chief interest in life
has been a general attempt to find God more easily in the world.
It's an all-consuming effort, but it's the only vocation I know as
my own, and nothing can turn me from it." [45] We are witnessing
today in Christian spirituality the fruits of this "all-consuming"
effort of Teilhard's life. What he has given is a coherent focus
for the modern Christian imagination, a focus open to every new
experience, yet supported by the deepest insights of the past.
His image of the world uniting men to Christ has reopened the
possibility of unity once more in Christian living. His vision of
Christ not only as the model of a fully human life but the source
and direction of history has strengthened hope in God and added
besides an all-encompassing hope in man. He has shown to Christians the seriousness of the world, and to non-Christians he has
carried the message that the world does not exclude God, that
adoration is an essential part of human life, and that union with
Christ means also union with the world.

IX

Method, Person and Marx

In this final chapter we shall briefly treat the thought of Pierre Teilhard de Chardin insofar as it impinges upon three movements in contemporary philosophy: phenomenology, personalism and Marxism. In each case it will become clear that, in spite of an apparent similarity in language and even to some extent in problematic, his evolutionary system is quite distinct from these movements. The system will, moreover, be seen to be basically religious both in inspiration and orientation. This religious dimension will not be dealt with directly, since Teilhard's philosophical thought, along with its premises and conclusions, can stand independent scrutiny and be judged alone. Yet the reader should be aware that such independent scrutiny will reveal gaps which can be filled in only on the level of Teilhard's theological speculation and personal religious experience.[1]

I

To raise the question of Teilhard's relationship to modern phenomenology is to pinpoint one of the major problem areas in his system of thought, the problem of classification. He himself called it at various times "phenomenology," "physics," "hyper-physics," "ultraphysics," "generalized physics." What he was searching for was a synthesis of knowledge which neither science nor philosophy had yet achieved, and this involved him in a criticism of both, the first for being too specialized, the second for losing contact with the physical world. Science, he said, has excluded from its considerations that which is proper to man, his power to think and to reflect, and has consequently been speaking about an inhuman and truncated world. Philosophy, on the other hand, while concentrating upon man, has ignored man's relationship to matter and has tended to construct an *a priori* and purely deductive knowledge starting from abstract principles and ideas.[2]

Teilhard's solution to this dilemma, which made impossible the type of synthesis he wanted, was to widen the range of pure science. For him this meant widening the concept of "phenomenon" to which pure science, by the rigors of its own methodology, sought to remain faithful. "We have knowledge of man on the fringe of the universe, but still no science of the universe including man as such. Present day physics (using the word in the broad Greek sense of a 'systematic comprehension of all nature') as yet makes no place for thought; which means it is still constructed wholly apart from the most remarkable of all phenomena provided by nature for our observation." [3]

Science, then, if it is to be true to its own methodology, must deal with man. "My book deals with the human phenomenon and that alone, but it deals with the *total* human phenomenon." [4] In order to come to terms with this total phenomenon, science must concern itself with questions which were formerly thought reserved for philosophy. This does not mean that there is to be a change in scientific method, but rather that this method is to be applied to areas of human life presumed until now to lie beyond the realm of phenomena. The result will be "a kind of phenomenology or generalized physics in which the internal aspect of things as well as the external aspect of the world will be taken into account. Otherwise, so it seems to me, it is impossible to cover the totality of the cosmic phenomenon by one coherent explanation as science must try to construct." [5] But why must it be science that widens its horizon? Why not philosophy? And why not modern phenomenology? Teilhard gave his reason in 1953 and it will be worth quoting at length:

I recognize that my "phenomenology" is not that of Husserl and Merleau-Ponty. But where can I find another word to define a *Weltanschauung* based on the study of the development of phenomena? We are forced to use the word "evolution" for theories very different from one another. In fact, if I understand them properly, it is rather the "phenomenologists" who usurp their title insofar as they appear to ignore one of the most essential dimensions of phenomena: not simply the power of being perceived by an individual consciousness but the added power of showing to that consciousness that it is part of a universal process of "noogenesis." I simply do not understand how anyone can call himself a "phenomenologist" and write whole books without even mentioning the words "cosmogenesis" and "evolution." [6]

The above text, as well as several others of a similar nature, makes it clear that Teilhard believed philosophers to be neither willing nor capable of doing what he wanted done. "I mistrust metaphysics (in the usual sense of the word) because I feel it to be a sort of geometry. But I am ready to recognize another kind of metaphysics, which would really be a hyper-physics or a hyper-biology." [7] Or again: "I should be happy to see you do what I am trying to do, that is, penetrate still further into spiritual and human questions by the use of the methods of science, substituting for the metaphysics of which we are dying an ultra-physics (the real *physike* of the Greeks, I imagine) where matter and spirit would be embraced in one single coherent and homogeneous explanation of the world." [8]

Now this effort to create a "phenomenology" which was neither science in the accepted sense nor philosophy, involved Teilhard in an epistemological bind that has been the source of much legitimate and sometimes severe criticism.[9] There is first his attempt to use scientific method in areas where statements about "phenomena" are unverifiable. How is one possibly to verify, for example, that an analysis of sidereal radiations from another planet would reveal to the observer the "phosphorescence of thought" covering our earth? [10] How can it be established "from the most coldly positivistic point of view" that thought is an envelope around the earth, "more vibrant, more conductive in a sense than any metal, more mobile than any fluid, more expansive than any vapor, with more capacity to assimilate and more sensitivity than any form of organized matter"? [11] Can it really be said that, "considered solely from the experimental aspect, consciousness reveals itself as a cosmic property of variable size subject to a global transformation"? [12] The extrapolation of Teilhard's famous law of complexity-consciousness, remarkable though it is as an insight into evolution, can scarcely be said to be verifiable by any scientific evidence. When he says that there are two types of energy operating in the world, "radial," drawing an element forward into structures of great complexity, and "tangential," linking an element to other elements on the same level of organization, the presumption is that there is some way of establishing a direct relation between them. But no scientifically verifiable criteria are ever provided even for the existence of radial energy. In point of fact it designates the internal causal element in evolutionary movement which is the key to Teilhard's whole system, but in no sense can it be called a phenomenon open to scientific verification.[13]

The second epistemological problem arises from the obvious fact that Teilhard seems even less concerned about rigorous philosophical analysis than he is about scientific evidence for the justification of his phenomenology. A case in point is again the existence of radial energy, which he calls the "within" of things, and which is responsible for the direction of evolution toward growth in consciousness.[14] When he says that "a certain mass of elementary consciousness was originally imprisoned in the matter of earth," his warrant is not any scientific evidence of the earth's behavior at the moment of its formation, but rather the eventual development of human interiority at a later period. "To make room for thought in the world I have had to 'interiorize' matter; to imagine an energetics of mind; to conceive a noogenesis rising upstream against the flow of entropy; to provide evolution with a direction, a line of advance and critical points." [15] Matter must somehow be conceived as possessing from the very beginning a "consciousness" analogous to human consciousness, and the tangential energy operating on the level of organization must be sufficiently analogous to that in human thinking to warrant calling both by the same name.

But how is this analogy justified? Certainly not by an elaborate prior analysis of human consciousness such as phenomenology would undertake. The priority here of idea over empirical evidence should reflect a theory of knowledge which would legitimize the imposition of certain categories of thought upon experience. Teilhard's lack of precision in defining his large number of neologisms makes it difficult to see how he applies these concepts to the physical world as science explains it. He might well have felt that the language of the physical scientist is too narrow to express what is taking place in the world. But one can then legitimately ask what are Teilhard's criteria to insure that when he and the scientist speak of "life," "energy," or "consciousness," they are speaking more or less about the same thing. The same holds true for his analogous use of the word "love" as applied both to human interpersonal relationships and to the union of elements on the level of pre-life and the pre-human. "Love," says Teilhard, is "the affinity of being with being. . . . If there were no propensity to unite, even at a prodigiously elementary level—indeed in the molecule itself—it would be physically impossible for love to appear higher up, with us, in 'hominized' form. By rights, to be certain of its presence in ourselves, we should assume its presence at least in an inchoate form, in everything that is." [16] And yet, more than one philosopher has suggested that the two languages are absolutely incommensurate, since Teilhard never really attempts either to "operationalize" his phenomenological analysis or give legitimate phenomenological significance to terms taken over from biology and physics.[17]

Yet if Teilhard uses neither scientific methodology (as he claims) nor rigorous philosophical analysis to justify his "phenomenology," what criteria does he use? "The success of the project as a whole is what will decide," he writes. "If a system of thought enables us to grasp a little more of the world and helps us better to harmonize its elements, we can be sure we are closer to the truth. . . . Truth is nothing but a total coherence of the universe in regard to each of its elements. . . . The truth about man is the truth of the universe for man. . . . Leaving aside useless discussion, let us look at the universe as positivists and see whether it is really coherent." . . . "Order and homogeneity, that is to say, truth." [18] These texts make it clear that the test of truth for Teilhard is coherence. Had he been pressed on this point (which he was not, since most of his writings were unpublished in his lifetime), he would probably have had to admit that of itself such a criterion could scarcely be sufficient, since it is obviously possible to have a coherent and ordered view of the world without using any of his categories of consciousness, love, energy, thought, etc.

Whether or not Teilhard's particular coherence imposes itself will consequently depend in the final analysis on whether one "sees" the world as he sees it, namely in his own evolutionary perspective and with its ultimate orientation toward a divine, personal Omega. It is no accident that the prologue to *The Phenomenon of Man* is entitled "Seeing," nor that Teilhard should warn the reader at the very start: "While this aura of subjective interpretation [in scientific explanations] may remain imperceptible where the field of observation is limited, it is bound to become practically dominant as soon as the field of vision extends to the whole. . . . This work may be summed up as an attempt to *see* and *to make others see*. . . . Object and subject unite and mutually transform each other in the act of knowledge; hence man willy-nilly finds his own image stamped on all he looks at." [19] In other words, objective data become coherent by reason of the prior options of the thinking subject.

In Teilhard's case, however, these prior options have their source neither in "phenomenology" (whether philosophic or Teilhardian) nor in the "phenomena" of the scientist, but in his belief in Christian revelation. In the last resort it was Christian faith which gave him his certitude that an Absolute existed and that this Absolute was responsible for beginning the evolutionary process and would infallibly bring it to completion in himself. "For the Christian believer . . . the final success of hominization (and thus cosmic coiling) is positively guaranteed by the power of restoring to life which belongs to God incarnate in his creation. But this takes us beyond the plane of phenomena." [20] And he admits quite candidly that the existence of a personal Omega was in fact motivated by the knowledge of Christ which he had through faith.[21] Both the scientist and the phenomenologist-philosopher have, then, a legitimate grievance against Teilhard when he claims that he alone is doing what science and philosophy should be doing, namely phenomenology. Let them look closer, however, and they will see that this phenomenology draws its ultimate epistemological stability neither from science nor philosophy, but from Christian revelation.

II

The point at issue we have just discussed in Teilhard's relationship to science and phenomenology, namely his desire for a synthetic knowledge of man as part of the evolutionary process, will help us situate his thought in relationship to a second philosophical movement, personalism. Teilhard's strong personalistic emphasis arises from his attempt "to build an understanding of the physical world around the human person as the determining element in the whole system. What kind of make-up and future are we going to assign to the cosmos, given the fact that the reflecting monad is at its center?" [22] The meaning of the world must thus coincide with the meaning of the person; to give meaning to one is to give meaning to the other, since the genetic development of both coincide. This explains why Teilhard takes so much pains to locate the human person within the evolutionary movement and then to show that it is precisely man's personality which makes him unique and gives him a certain autonomy in the material world.

Teilhard's first intention is clearly to show the meaning which evolution gives to man. The direction of evolution, according to his law of complexity-consciousness, can be judged by following the line of growing complexity, a line which has gradually made its way through only one zoological group, namely that of the vertebrates, moving through mammals and primates up to man. "Because the specific orthogenesis of the primates (urging them towards increasing cerebralization) coincides with the axial orthogenesis of organized matter (urging all living things towards higher consciousness), man, appearing at the heart of the primates, flourishes on the leading shoot of zoological evolution." [23] Teilhard is thus affirming that the world is a unity and that a single pattern runs through the whole up to man.

More importantly, however, he is affirming that the phenomenon of reflective consciousness is totally unlike any other event in the evolutionary series, since for the first time a part of the cosmos found itself "personalized." "People usually speak of person as if it represented some quantitative reduction or qualitative diminishment of total reality. Exactly the opposite is the way we shall have to understand person. The 'personal' is the highest state in which we are privileged to grasp the stuff of the universe. . . . The only way to express in a phrase the fact that the world advances without retreating or losing any part of itself, is to say that the quantity and quality of the personal must constantly go on increasing." [24] It should be noted, moreover, that Teilhard's emphasis upon a unity of development from the chemical and biological up to the spiritual is in no sense a reduction of man to the biological or chemical. On the contrary, it is an assertion that only by focusing upon man can the material world and its destiny be properly understood. For man is not simply hominization (his original appearance on the earth) but the whole of his history as well as what can be projected regarding his future development.

The genesis of the human phenomenon from nature is thus merely a first moment in Teilhard's dialectic; the second moment shows man giving meaning to the whole process and acting as a spearhead. The fact that each level of development comes from the preceding does not mean that it is fully explained by the preceding. This is why Teilhard's theory of "critical points" is extremely important, since these always mark a profound change in nature by which something totally new is produced. In the case of man this is his "personality," his power of reflection and self-determination. "What is the work of works for man if not to establish, in and by men as of each one of us, an absolutely original center, in which the universe reflects itself in a unique and inimitable way? And those centers are precisely ourselves, our personalities." [25] Man's power freely to choose his destiny is therefore not absolute, but is conditioned by the situation in which a particular man or group of men find themselves at any given point in evolutionary development.

Now the objection has been raised that Teilhard's approach to personality, by placing a strong emphasis upon man's continuity with all other living beings, makes it extremely difficult to attribute to him that dignity which the human person demands. This is what emerged in 1963 and 1964, when two whole issues of *Esprit* dealt with the problem of personalism in Teilhard. The editor, Jean-Marie Domenach, was quite explicit in his opinion that Teilhard's thought was ultimately incompatible with that of Emmanuel Mounier, in spite of the warm personal friendship between the two men.[26] It becomes clear, however, from reading Domenach, that his main objection is not so much Teilhard's emphasis on man's continuity with lower forms, but rather the fact that in Teilhard's synthesis the person can only reach fulfillment in a collectivity. This is indeed a central assertion in Teilhard's system and it would be well for us to clarify it now.

As is well known, Teilhard believed that the evolutionary forces at work for millions of years did not cease to operate with the appearance of man. Rather their development continues to take place in the noosphere, that mysterious realm of the person and of interpersonal communion. "The social phenomenon is the culmination and not the attenuation of the biological phenomenon." [27] "Socialization" in Teilhard's sense of the term is a slow process of "collective cerebralization" in which the law of complexity-consciousness continues to operate in the same way as it formerly did in the case of individual cerebralization before the coming of thought. To what extent this socialization should result in a "harmonized collectivity of consciousness" is open to some dispute, but what is beyond doubt is the fact that such "totalization," as he also calls it, involves the perfection of all the personal elements precisely insofar as they are persons. "It is a mistake to look for the extension of our being in the impersonal. . . . In any domain—whether it be the cells of a body, the members of a society or the elements of a spiritual synthesis—*union differentiates*. In every organized whole the parts perfect themselves and fulfill themselves." The dichotomy between totalization and personalization is the result of confusing individuality with personality. "The peak of ourselves, the acme of our originality, is not our individuality but our person; and according to the evolutionary structure of the world we can only find our person by uniting together. . . . Totalization and personalization are two expressions of a single movement. . . . Socialization means not the end but rather the beginning of the Era of the Person." [28]

The operative phrase in all these quotations is "union differentiates," repeated frequently in Teilhard's writings.[29] By this he means that true union, based upon love energy, personalizes, and the more all-encompassing the union the greater the degree of personalization. This concept of differentiating union Teilhard opposes to all forms of modern totalitarianism where love has no significant role to play at all. All these movements toward collectivity, he felt, were really distortions of an energy fundamental to human life and therefore quite near the truth. "Although our individualistic instincts may rebel against the drive towards the collective, they do so in vain and wrongly. In vain because no power in the world can enable us to escape from what is in itself the power of the world. And wrongly because the real nature of this impulse that is sweeping us towards a state of super-organization is such as to make us more completely personalized and human." [30]

This brief summary of Teilhard's position will enable us better to evaluate the main objection of Domenach and other personalists, namely that the biological phenomenon whereby cells unite and solidify without deterioration cannot be equated with the social phenomenon, since the human person is of a totally different order from the cells of an organism.[31] Teilhard's answer is to insist once more that man's continuity with lower forms means that the realities expressed by terms such as radial and tangential energy can be verified equally, though analogically, in the personal as well as in the material. What in man we call love or interpersonal communion appears on the lower levels as that attraction between atoms and molecules responsible for all organic development. Consequently something analogous to molecularization is going on at the level of society (socialization is Teilhard's word for it), and this of itself need in no way be derogatory to the human person as person. Such an analogical use of the word love, it is interesting to note, has been defended from a scientific point of view by the neurophysiologist Paul

Chauchard, as well as from a sociological point of view by Pitirim Sorokin.[32]

Once more, however, we must recognize the ultimately religious basis of this unshakable conviction that the person will not in the end be injured by the collectivity. The whole theme of personalism in Teilhard is a reflection within his evolutionary system of the relationship he himself experienced with the Person of Christ. In the last analysis his is "a personalistic universe," to use his own English expression, because he sees Christ as the *real* (as opposed to the hypothetical) Omega of evolution, and as such the physical Center of all the fibers of the universe. His knowledge as a Christian that all men were destined at the end of time to be united with the Body-Person of Christ, was in fact what led him to speak with such assurance of a *super-* and *hyper-*consciousness to come, a collective act of reflection in which man will reach perfection as a person. "The task of the world consists not in engendering in itself some supreme reality but in bringing itself to fulfillment through union with a pre-existent Being." [33] The biological reality is thus illuminated by the religious reality, and the impersonal aspect of collectivity by the ultimate spiritual destiny of mankind. It is the Person of Christ as the source of love energy in the world who guarantees that the collective should be the completer and not the destroyer of the person.

III

The emphasis placed by Teilhard upon the full development of the human person will enable us more easily to see the similarity as well as the strong contrast between his thought and Marxism. The similarity has been pointed out frequently enough, most strikingly by the French Marxist Roger Garaudy.[34] While insisting that Teilhard has only a very elementary knowledge of Marxist philosophy, Garaudy readily acknowledges that he has incorporated into a Christian synthesis much of the Marxist enthusiasm for man's future aspirations and hopes. "Even on the level of devotion to the world," wrote Teilhard a few weeks before he died in 1955, "I can say rightfully and with pride to my humanist or Marxist comrade: *plus et ego.*" [35] Much earlier, in 1927, he had written in a similar vein of the Christian concern for the human: "How could we be deserters or sceptics about the future of the tangible world? How could we be repelled by human work? How little you know us! You suspect us of not sharing your concern and your hopes and your excitement. . . . You are men, you say? *Plus et ego.*" [36]

For Teilhard, then, as for the Marxist, there is a pressing demand upon men today to dedicate themselves to human progress. "I feel resolutely determined," he wrote in 1941, "to devote myself by all possible means to the defense of the idea and the reality of a progress (collective and personalizing) against every secular and religious pessimism." [37] Like Marx, he too was concerned with changing the world, not simply discussing it. Marxism is thus presented with an understanding of Christianity which places a central emphasis upon building the earthly city. Far from being an opiate, the Christian religion becomes for Teilhard a driving force, whose doctrine of love provides the key not only to Christian action, but also to the whole movement of evolution, since love is the highest form of radial energy in the noosphere. Teilhard felt Christianity to be in fact the source of this love energy, and spoke of it as a phylum of love inserted by God into the human phylum in order to guarantee that humanity reach the fullness of its development toward planetary maturation. The whole dynamism of Teilhard's thinking as well as of his life is thus a refutation of Marx's statement that it is easy to become a saint if one does not want to be a man.

"What constitutes the contagious strength of Marxism is the illegitimate monopolizing of the *sense* of evolution," he wrote in 1954.[38] This "sense" he felt to be better explained by Christianity. Both Christian and Marxist, however, must recognize the full significance of the two currents of psychic energy which characterize the action and thinking of modern man. Teilhard called these two currents "faiths," one being the Christian faith in a personal God which is directed "upward," the other being human faith in progress and the primacy of man which is directed "forward." The real drama in the present religious conflict is the apparent impossibility of reconciling these upward and forward movements. "On one side we have spiritualists (especially Christians), whose faith in God seems to immunize them from any hope or even any desire to bring about some form of super-humanity, and on the other side we have 'materialists' (especially Marxists) who regard any appeal to transcendent finality as compromising and derogatory to their faith in man." [39] What has to be done is to synthesize these two faiths, not by compromising either, but by combining them into a single resultant energy, reinforcing one faith by the other. The Christian must open himself to the world and human progress, and the Marxist must open himself to the spiritual.

The key to this mutual opening was to be found, Teilhard felt, in his own evolutionary system. This system postulated a simultaneity between the point of planetary maturation and the point of the Parousia of Christ; the first being the summit of faith in man, the second the fulfillment of faith in Christ. Just as the first coming of Christ demanded that men have reached a certain anatomical and social development, so his second coming at the end of time would seem to demand that the human species as a whole has already reached its full natural development in order to be able to receive from Christ its supernatural consummation. "The point of human maturation" would thus be "a condition (not indeed sufficient and determinative, but necessary)" for "the point of the Parousia." [40] If these two foci in fact coincide, then there should be no radical opposition between the two movements to which they give rise. "Some (the old-fashioned Christians) say: Await the return of Christ. Others (the Marxists) reply: Achieve the World. And the third (the neo-Catholics) think: In order that Christ can return we must *achieve* the World." [41]

Nevertheless, in spite of its power to reduce the distance between the two "faiths" at the level of human action, Teilhard's conceptual framework contains elements which contrast strongly with Marxism. Teilhard had no intention, for example, of simply adding a Christian dimension to Marxism, or of claiming that it is simply the beginning of a curve which is to be completed by Christianity. In the synthesis of these two faiths the

Christian movement "upward" does not become immersed in the human movement "forward," but rather transforms it along with all the elements that make it up. The reason for this is that in evolution it is the terminus which determines the nature of all that moves toward it. And for Teilhard this terminus of evolution, namely the collective consummation of humanity, is not an infra-temporal millennium but a very precise moment at the end of time, the moment when the psychic temperature of the noosphere, in conformity with the law of complexity-consciousness, reaches its maximum of tension. Hence the importance in Teilhard's system of what he calls "the hominization of death," by which he means the Christian teaching on transformation and rebirth as it has been incorporated into his own thinking.

Now it is this conviction that the human person can reach full development only by an escape from the "time-space matrix," which places Teilhard's thought in sharpest contrast with Marxism by giving a totally different perspective to man's commitment to human values. For these values are now seen to be directed not toward an indefinite progress, which would contradict Teilhard's understanding of the convergent nature of noogenesis, but toward a paroxysm of human freedom transcending the dimensions of the visible universe. There is not therefore a question of the "well-being" of humanity at the end of the evolutionary process, but a question of "more-being." True spiritual progress obviously means an improvement of man's economic condition in the world, but to attribute any ultimate stability to such improvement must eventually lead to what Teilhard called "Marxism's depersonalizing action." [42] To confuse an expectation of "more-being" with that of mere "well-being" is to do away completely with any hope of a way out from the world, and thereby imprison man in an absurd universe where death would be the end of everything. The English astronomer Sir James Jeans was sharply criticized by Teilhard precisely because he offered man the hope that life on earth would go on for millions of years. "In the face of a death which was absolute and sure, what difference does it make to our taste for life whether it be one year or a million million years!" [43]

Consequently within Teilhard's system the Marxist commitment to human values is radically deficient. "You Marxists do not go far enough in fostering simply the 'forward' development of man!" [44] Man cannot agree to work toward total death, either individual or collective. He carries within him a need for life and love which cannot be uprooted. "The radical defect of all forms of belief in progress, as they are expressed in positivist credos, is that they do not eliminate death. What is the use of detecting a focus of any sort in the van of evolution if that focus can and must disintegrate?" [45] Hence the crucial importance of belief in a divine, personal Center for evolution, whose existence here and now is alone capable of guaranteeing evolution's success. This supreme personal Center is in turn the real object of man's desire for survival, a desire which for Teilhard is the mainspring of all human activity. By transcending death, the God of Christianity is alone capable of saving the work of humanity and consequently bringing man's movement "forward" to a successful terminus.

The purpose of this chapter has been briefly to situate the thought of Teilhard against three movements in modern philosophy, phenomenology, personalism and Marxism. Teilhard's concern for these areas reflects what are perhaps the dominant preoccupations of modern man, a concern for the material, for the personal, and for the future. Though he himself was not a philosopher by profession, and the totality of his work cannot be called philosophy in the strict sense, his total vision of life does indeed contain a philosophical dimension which cannot be ignored. Its great strength lies in his attempt to restore a truly human significance to the universe, and to make the world of science not only begin with man but take its significance from man. A sterile, compartmentalized science, cut off from its phenomenological roots, can never exert any influence upon man's future. For this future is coming to be more and more centered upon man's capacity to control his destiny and to overcome the anxiety which characterizes his present outlook. [46] In spite of the absence of a developed and critical phenomenology, Teilhard's evolutionary system elaborates an option for hope, a "faith" as he himself called it, which combines with his faith as a Christian to give a unified and optimistic vision of man. It was humanity that he loved and it was in the victory of humanity that he believed. "I wonder whether today," he once wrote, "humanity is not really in the process of being split between those who believe and those who do not believe in the future of the universe. And I feel more decidedly than ever that I must line up with the former, for the conquest of the world." [47]

Notes

NOTES FOR INTRODUCTION

1. Bernard Lonergan, "Theology in Its New Context," *Theology of Renewal,* vol. 1, ed. L. K. Shook (New York, 1968), 41.
2. John Courtney Murray, "Toward a Christian Humanism," *A Philosophical Symposium on American Catholic Education* (New York, 1941), 111-112.
3. Ephesians 2, 10.
4. *Summa Theologica,* II-II, 163, 2; *De Malo,* 16, 3.
5. John Courtney Murray, "The Roman Catholic Church," *The Annals of the American Academy of Political and Social Science,* CCLVI (1948), 41.
6. A. Dwight Culler, *The Imperial Intellect* (New Haven, 1955), 241.
7. Karl Rahner, "Current Problems in Christology," *Theological Investigations,* vol. 1 (Baltimore, 1961), 184.
8. Edward Schillebeeckx, *God the Future of Man* (New York, 1968), 72.
9. Michael Ramsey, "The Idea of the Holy and the World Today," *Spirituality for Today,* ed. Eric James (London, 1968), 138. See also in the same collection the paper by John B. Coburn, "The New Mood in Spirituality."
10. Romans 8, 57.
11. 1 Corinthians 1, 30.
12. Letter of September 26, 1900, in *Baron Friedrich von Hügel: Selected Letters, 1896-1924,* ed. B. Holland (New York, 1927), 88, 96. This theme in von Hügel has been developed at length by Joseph P. Whelan in an unpublished doctoral dissertation at London University, *The Spiritual Doctrine of Friedrich von Hügel as Found in His Writings.*
13. John Macquarrie, "Self-Transcending Man," *Commonweal,* XCI (1969), 155.

NOTES FOR CHAPTER I

1. *Pastoral Constitution on the Church in the Modern World,* art. 40, 41. All quotations from Council documents are taken from Walter M. Abbot, editor, *The Documents of Vatican II* (New York, 1966).

2. *Ibid.*
3. *Ibid.*, art. 4.
4. *Ibid.*, art. 55.
5. Karl Rahner, *The Church after the Council* (New York, 1966), 93.
6. *Pastoral Constitution*, art. 62.
7. *Ibid.*, art. 5.
8. Yves Congar, in his paper at the Marxist-Christian Congress at Marienbad, April 28, 1967, soon to be published in the proceedings, *Schöpfertum und Freiheit.*
9. Bernard Lonergan, "The Dehellenization of Dogma," *Theological Studies*, XXVII (1967), 347.
10. See the development of these remarks by Robert C. Neville, "Current Issues in Christian Ecumenism," *World Order*, III (1968), 30-34.
11. Christian Duquoc, "Theology and Spirituality," *Concilium*, vol. XIX, *Spirituality in the Secular City* (New York, 1966), 97.
12. *Pastoral Constitution*, art. 19.
13. *Ibid.*, art. 21.
14. Gabriel Marcel, *Problematic Man* (New York, 1967), 54.
15. Bernard Lonergan, "Theology in Its New Context," *Theology of Renewal*, vol. I, ed. L. K. Shook (New York, 1968), 34-46. See especially 44-45.
16. Teilhard's thought on this problem is developed at greater length in Chapter VII.
17. *Pastoral Constitution*, art. 39.
18. *Ibid.*, art. 38.
19. See Johannes Metz, "The Responsibility of Hope," *Philosophy Today*, X (1966), 280-281.
20. *Pastoral Constitution*, art. 37.
21. Jürgen Moltmann, "Resurrection as Hope," *Harvard Theological Review*, LXI (1968), 146-147.
22. Lonergan, "Theology in Its New Context," 41.
23. *Pastoral Constitution*, art. 38.
24. *Ibid.*, art. 22.
25. *Ibid.*, art. 41.
26. This cosmic role of Christ and its relationship to his role as Savior has been elaborated at great length in the theology of Teilhard de Chardin. See Christopher F. Mooney, *Teilhard de Chardin and the Mystery of Christ* (New York, 1966), 67-145.
27. See on this question Edward Schillebeeckx, "The Church and Mankind," *Concilium*, vol. I, *The Church and Mankind* (New York, 1965), 69-101.
28. *Pastoral Constitution*, art. 36.
29. *Ibid.*, art. 54.
30. *Ibid.*, art. 58.

31. Bernard Lonergan, *Collection* (New York, 1967), 266-267.
32. Julian Hartt, *A Christian Critique of American Culture* (New York, 1967), xviii.
33. Edward Schillebeeckx, *Revelation and Theology*, vol. I (New York, 1967), 161. See the same author's *The Real Achievement of Vatican II* (New York, 1967), 88-90.

NOTES FOR CHAPTER II

1. Romano Guardini, *Prayer in Practice* (London, 1957), 94-95
2. *Summa Theologica,* I, 3, prologue.
3. *De Potentia Dei,* 7, 5, ad 14.
4. Karl Rahner, "The 'Commandment' of Love in Relation to the Other Commandments," *Theological Investigations,* vol. 5 (Baltimore, 1966), 452.
5. Luke 21, 36.
6. 1 John 3, 2.
7. Exodus 20, 2.
8. Isaiah 43, 18ff; 63, 15—64, 11.
9. 2 Corinthians 1, 20.
10. John 14, 26.
11. 1 Corinthians 4, 7.
12. Cf. Genesis, 1, 28.
13. Cf. 1 Corinthians 3, 9; Ephesians 4, 13.
14. 1 Corinthians 13, 11.
15. Philippians 2, 13.
16. Peter Baelz, *Prayer and Providence* (New York, 1968), 100.
17. Ephesians 3, 20.
18. D. Z. Phillips, *The Concept of Prayer* (London, 1965), 130.
19. Søren Kierkegaard, *The Sickness unto Death* (Princeton, 1941), 62-63.
20. Jürgen Moltmann, "The Realism of Hope," *Concordia Theological Monthly,* XL (1969), 152.
21. Phillips, *op. cit.,* 102.
22. Galatians 6, 15.
23. Herbert Butterfield, *Christianity and History* (London, 1949), 67.

NOTES FOR CHAPTER III

1. As reported in *The New York Times* for November 12 and 13, 1968.

2. Pierre Teilhard de Chardin, *The Phenomenon of Man* (New York, 1959), 229.

3. Peter L. Berger, "A Sociological View of the Secularization of Theology," *Journal for the Scientific Study of Religion,* VI (1967), 3-16. See also *The Sacred Canopy* (New York, 1967).

4. Edward Schillebeeckx, "Theology of Renewal Talks about God," *Theology of Renewal,* vol. I, ed. L. K. Shook, (New York, 1968), 98.

5. Schillebeeckx (*op. cit.,* 100) notes that this is the explicit teaching of Thomas Aquinas in *Summa Theologica,* I, 1, 7, ad 2. It is, moreover, commonly admitted today that all revelation is functional, that God reveals himself only in what he is for us and does for us in history.

6. *Ibid.,* 95-96.

7. Jürgen Moltmann, *Theology of Hope* (New York, 1967); "Hope without Faith," *Concilium,* vol. XVI, *Is God Dead?* (New York, 1966), 25-40; "Hoping and Planning," *Cross Currents,* XVIII (1968), 307-318; "Hope and Confidence," *Dialog,* VII (1968), 42-55; "The Category of the New in Christian Theology," *The Future as the Presence of Shared Hope,* ed. Maryellen Muckenhirn (New York, 1968), 9-33; "Resurrection as Hope," *Harvard Theological Review,* LXI (1968), 129-148.

8. Wolfhart Pannenberg, *Jesus—God and Man* (Philadelphia, 1968); "Hope as the Arrival of the Future," *Journal of the American Academy of Religion,* XXXV (1967), 107-118; "Response to the Discussion," *Theology as History,* ed. James M. Robinson and John B. Cobb, Jr. (New York, 1967), 221-276; "Theology and the Kingdom of God," *Una Sancta,* XXIV (1967), 283-294.

9. Edward Schillebeeckx, *God the Future of Man* (New York, 1968), esp. Chapter 6, "Secularization and Man's Future on Earth."

10. Karl Rahner, "Building the New Earth," *Dialogue,* I (1968), 58-63; "Christentum als Religion der absoluten Zukunft," *Christentum und Marxismus Heute,* ed. Erich Kellner (Vienna, 1966), 202-213; "Experiment: Man," *Theology Digest,* Sesquicentennial Issue, February 1968, 57-69.

11. Johannes Metz, *Theology of the World* (New York, 1969); "The Responsibility of Hope," *Philosophy Today,* X (1966), 280-288; "Creative Hope," *Cross Currents,* XVII (1967), 171-180; "Religion and Society in the Light of a Political Theology," *Harvard Theological Review,* LXI (1968), 507-523.

12. Harvey Cox, *On Not Leaving It to the Snake,* (New York, 1967).

13. Ernst Bloch, *Das Prinzip Hoffnung* (Frankfurt, 1959).

14. Pierre Teilhard de Chardin, *The Future of Man* (New York, 1964).

15. Pannenberg, "The God of Hope," 286-287.

16. Pannenberg, "Theology and the Kingdom of God," 5.

17. Moltmann, *Theology of Hope,* 180.
18. Pannenberg, *Jesus—God and Man,* 24-28.
19. Moltmann, *Theology of Hope,* 201.
20. Moltmann, "Hope and Confidence," 52-54.
21. Pannenberg, "The God of Hope," 289-290.
22. Pannenberg, "Theology and the Kingdom of God," 9.
23. *Ibid.,* 11-12.
24. Moltmann, *Theology of Hope,* 20, 33.
25. Moltmann, "Hope Without Faith," 39.
26. Moltmann, "The Category of the New in Theology," 14, 24.
27. Moltmann, *Theology of Hope,* 18. With his usual perception, Philip Hefner concludes a discussion of this question by noting that "contradiction can only refer to the fact that our predictions and visions of those open possibilities are never adequate to the way in which the future actually unfolds." See "Questions for Moltmann and Pannenberg," *Una Sancta,* XXV (1968), 37.
28. Pannenberg, *Theology as History,* 267, note 77.
29. Metz, "The Responsibility of Hope," 284-287; Rahner, "Building the New Earth," 61-63.
30. Metz, "Creative Hope," 175-180.
31. Metz, "Religion and Society in the Light of a Political Theology," 507.
32. *Ibid.,* 512-515.
33. Schillebeeckx, *God the Future of Man,* 191.
34. *Ibid.,* 196.
35. Teilhard de Chardin, *The Future of Man,* 223-224, 267-268; on his use of "preliminary sketch" (*ébauche*), see *L'Energie Humaine* (Paris, 1962), 76, 81, 83, 171, 192.
36. Cox, *On Not Leaving It to the Snake,* 8-9, 40.
37. See Moltmann, *Theology of Hope,* 156ff; Pannenberg, *Jesus—God and Man,* 44ff. Heinrich Fries has underscored this criticism in "Spero ut Intelligam: Bemerkungen zu einer Theologie der Hoffnung," *Wahrheit und Verkündigung* (Paderborn, 1967), 368-372.
38. Rahner, "Experiment: Man," 62-66.
39. *Pastoral Constitution on the Church in the Modern World,* art. 31.
40. Schillebeeckx, *God the Future of Man,* 200.
41. Teilhard de Chardin, *The Future of Man,* 224-225.

NOTES FOR CHAPTER IV

1. A major contribution to this discussion is a recent study by Avery R. Dulles, "Dogma as an Ecumenical Problem," *Theological Studies,* XXIX (1968), 397-416.

2. These ideas are developed at greater length in Christopher F. Mooney, "College Theology and Liberal Education," *Thought,* XXXIV (1959), 325-330.

3. Zbigniew Brzezinski, "The Search for Meaning amid Change," *New York Times,* January 6, 1969, 147.

4. George Lindbeck, "Ecumenism and the Future of Belief," *Una Sancta,* XXV (1968), 11.

5. *Ibid.*

6. Confer the as yet unpublished plan for such an introductory course elaborated at Fordham University over several years and in substantial detail by L. Augustine Grady.

7. See Fergal McGrath, *Newman's University* (New York, 1951), 277, note 1, and 291, note 2.

8. *Declaration on Religious Freedom,* art. 10; *Pastoral Constitution on the Church in the Modern World,* art. 17. Quoted from *The Documents of Vatican II,* ed. Walter M. Abbot (New York, 1966).

9. John Henry Newman, *The Idea of a University,* Lecture V (Longmans edition, New York, 1939), 121.

NOTES FOR CHAPTER V

1. Henri Rondet has given a good summary of the Church's thought up to the present century: "Eléments pour une théologie de la femme," *Nouvelle Revue Théologique,* LXXXIX (1957), 915-940. In its original form this chapter appeared in *Woman in Modern Life,* ed. William C. Bier, and is reprinted here with the permission of Fordham University Press.

2. William B. Faherty has treated their thought at length in *The Destiny of Modern Woman in the Light of Papal Teaching* (Westminster, 1950), 10-108.

3. See Pius XII's allocution to working women on August 11, 1945, *Acta Apostolica Sedis,* XXXVII (1945), 213-217.

4. On these laws concerning the protection of woman, see P. M. Soullard, "Le Status de la femme dans l'Eglise," *Lumière et Vie,* VIII (1959), 53-64.

5. See Pius XII's allocution of October 14, 1956, to the Centre Feminin International de l'Action Catholique in *Acta Apostolica Sedis,* XLVIII (1956), 779-786.

6. John XXIII, "La Femme au foyer et au travail," allocution of December 7, 1960, in *Nouvelle Revue Théologique,* LXXXIII (1961) 295-297; encyclical letter, *Pacem in Terris,* no. 41.

7. Karl Barth develops this point in his *The Doctrine of Creation* (Edinburgh, 1958), 183-187, 313-316.

8. See Xavier Tilliette, "La Femme et la féminité," *La Femme, Nature et Vocation* (Paris, 1963), 116-118.

9. These ideas have been developed at length by Gertrud von le Fort, *The Eternal Woman* (Milwaukee, 1954), 33-46 and by Edith Stein, *Die Frau* (Freiburg, 1959), 1-15.

10. Gertrud von le Fort, *op. cit.*, 47-51. See also A. M. Henry, "Le Mystère de l'homme et de la femme," *La Vie Spirituelle*, LXXX (1949), 467-475.

11. "The mutual attraction of the sexes is so fundamental a fact," he says, "that any explanation of the world which does not succeed in incorporating it structurally, as an essential part of its edifice, is virtually condemned." Confer *L'Energie humain* (Paris, 1962), 91.

12. *Ibid.*, 94. Catherine O'Connor has treated with great thoroughness this whole aspect of Teilhard's thought in *Woman and Cosmos: The Feminine in the Thought of Teilhard de Chardin*, an unpublished doctoral dissertation recently defended at Fordham University.

13. *Ibid.*, 93.

14. *Le Coeur de la matière*, 33, an unpublished essay written in 1950. Confer also *L'Energie humain*, 40-42, 131-134.

15. Mary's role in the economy of salvation is treated at length in the *Dogmatic Constitution on the Church*, art. 52-69.

16. *Pastoral Constitution on the Church in the Modern World*, art. 29. A fascinating historical note, however, is the exceptional exercise of what would seem to have been spiritual jurisdiction by certain medieval abbesses who were allowed to wear the mitre and accept the homage of the local clergy. On this see Mary Daly, *The Church and the Second Sex* (New York, 1968), 54.

17. The article "Women in the Church," *Herder Correspondence*, VI (1969), 291-298, gives all the pertinent background to this question as well as references to current literature.

18. Jean Daniélou, "Le Ministère des femmes dans l'Eglise ancienne," *La Maison-Dieu*, LXI (1960), 70-96. Romans 16, 1-2 is an explicit reference to the deaconess Phoebe; 1 Timothy 3, 8-13 seems to be a list of qualifications for the office of deaconess as well as deacon; and Evodia and Syntyche of Philippians 4, 2-3 may well have been deaconess at Philippi.

19. See the commentary of Jean Héring, *La Première épitre de Saint Paul aux Corinthians* (Paris, 1949), 130. Exegetes have in general been puzzled by the inconsistency in Paul's statements on women in chapters 11 and 14, some claiming that verses 34-35

of chapter 14 are an interpolation in the text. Confer also Krister Stendahl, *The Bible and the Role of Women* (Philadelphia, 1966), 30.

20. Karl Rahner, "Notes on the Lay Apostolate," *Theological Investigations,* vol. II (Baltimore, 1963), 349.

21. *Ibid.,* 341-342.

22. Abel Jeannière, *The Anthropology of Sex* (New York, 1967), 126-173.

23. Daly, *op. cit.,* 147-148.

NOTES FOR CHAPTER VI

1. This point has been developed by Walter Dirks, *The Monk and the World* (New York, 1954).

2. *Monumenta Ignatiana, Series Prima, Epistolae et Instructiones,* vol. I (Rome, 1903), 72 and 101. Confer François Courel, "Saint Ignace et la gloire plus grande de Dieu," *Christus,* III (1956), 328-348.

3. Hugo Rahner, "Esprit et Eglise, un chapitre de théologie ignatienne," *Christus,* V (1958), 163-184.

4. *Monumenta Ignatiana, Series Prima, Epistolae et Instructiones,* vol. IV (Rome, 1906), 126.

5. *Ibid.,* vol. II (Rome, 1904), 234.

6. Emerich Coreth, "In Actione Contemplativus," *Zeitschrift für Katholische Theologie,* LXXVI (1954), 55-82.

7. *Monumenta Ignatiana, Series Tertia, Constitutiones,* vol. I (Rome, 1934), 86-158. An English translation of this remarkable document has been made by William J. Young, *Woodstock Letters,* LXXXVII (1958), 195-267.

8. Joseph de Guibert, "Charactères de la mystique ignatienne," *La Spiritualité de la Compagnie de Jésus* (Rome, 1953), 33-42. It was also Eucharistic, as the same author makes clear, but this aspect will be seen more clearly later in this chapter.

9. *Monumenta Ignatiana, Series Quarta, Scripta de Sancto Ignatio de Loyola,* vol. I (Rome, 1904), 418.

10. *Constitution on the Sacred Liturgy,* art. 12. See also *Mediator Dei,* no. 37; in nn. 28-36 there is a further development of this same point, as well as in nn. 178-80, where the Holy Father treats explicitly of the Spiritual Exercises.

11. This subject has been treated at length by John N. Schumacher, "Ignatian Spirituality and the Liturgy," *Woodstock Letters,* LXXXVII (1958), 14-35.

12. *Acta Apostolica Sedis,* XXXVIII (1946), 149.

13. Karl Rahner, "Die ignatianische Mystik der Weltfreudigkeit," *Schriften zur Theologie,* vol. III (Einsiedeln, 1957), 329-348.

NOTES FOR CHAPTER VII

1. Gabriel Vahanian, *No Other God* (New York, 1966), 32.
2. *Pastoral Constitution on the Church in the Modern World,* art. 11, in Walter M. Abbot, editor, *The Documents of Vatican II* (New York, 1966).
3. *Le Goût de vivre,* 1950, in *L'Activation de l'énergie* (Paris, 1963), 248.
4. *Quelques réflexions sur la conversion du monde,* 1936, in *Science et Christ* (Paris, 1965), 164. [Eng. trans., *Science and Christ* (New York, 1968), 125.]
5. *Le Coeur du problème,* 1949, in *L'Avenir de l'homme* (Paris, 1959), 339. [Eng. trans., *The Future of Man* (New York, 1964), 260.]
6. *Quelques réflexions sur la conversion du monde,* 1936, in *Science et Christ,* 160. [Eng. trans., 121.]
7. *Note pour servir à l'évangelisation des temps nouveaux,* 1919, in *Ecrits du temps de la guerre* (Paris, 1965), 380. This essay does not appear in the English translation of this work.
8. *Mon univers,* 1924, in *Science et Christ,* 66. [Eng. trans., 38.]
9. *Comment je crois,* 1934, 1-2. An unpublished essay.
10. Letter of June 13, 1936, in *Lettres de voyage* (Paris, 1956), 207. [Eng. trans., *Letters of a Traveller* (New York, 1962), 226.]
11. *Introduction à la vie chrétienne,* 1944, 2. An unpublished essay.
12. *Mon univers,* 1924, in *Science et Christ,* 67. [Eng. trans., 39.]
13. *La Foi en l'homme,* 1947, in *L'Avenir de l'homme,* 243. [Eng. trans., 192.]
14. References to most of these essays will be found in the second chapter of Christopher F. Mooney, *Teilhard de Chardin and the Mystery of Christ* (New York, 1966), 34-66.
15. *Sur l'existence probable, en avant de nous, d'un "ultra-humain,"* 1950, in *L'Avenir de l'homme,* 361-362. [Eng. trans., 277-278.]
16. On Teilhard and Marxism, see Chapter IX.
17. *Comment concevoir et espérer que se réalise sur terre l'unanimisation humaine?,* 1950, in *L'Avenir de l'homme,* 373. [Eng. trans., 286.]
18. *Barrière de la mort et co-réflexion,* 1955, in *L'Activation de l'énergie,* 425-426.
19. *Comment concevoir et espérer que se réalise sur terre l'unanimisa-*

tion humaine?, 1950, in *L'Avenir de l'homme,* 373-374. [Eng. trans., 286-288.]

20. "On the strictly psychological plane . . . I mean by 'faith' any adherence of our intelligence to a general view of the universe. . . . *To believe is to achieve an intellectual synthesis." Comment je crois,* 1934, 2. An unpublished essay.

21. *La Formation de la noosphere,* 1947, in *L'Avenir de l'homme,* 228. [Eng. trans., 181.]

22. Letter of May 11, 1923, in *Lettres de voyage,* 31. [Eng. trans., 70-71.]

23. Letter of October 18, 1940, in *Lettres de voyage,* 262. [Eng. trans., 269.]

24. See, for example, *Le Phénomène humain* (Paris, 1955), 297. [Eng. trans., *The Phenomenon of Man* (New York, 1959), 267.]

25. On the importance of Teilhard's distinction between individual and person in his own system, see Mooney, *Mystery,* 46, 179-180.

26. *Le Phénomène humain,* 299-300. [Eng. trans., 269.]

27. *Comment je vois,* 1948, 14. An unpublished essay.

28. Text cited by Claude Cuénot, *Teilhard de Chardin* (Baltimore, 1965), 391.

29. *Le Phénomène humain,* 301. [Eng. trans., 270.] *Esquisse d'une dialectique de l'esprit,* in *L'Activation de l'énergie,* 152.

30. *Note sur les modes de l'action divine dans l'univers,* 1920, 4. An unpublished essay.

31. *Le Paradoxe transformiste,* 1925, in *La Vision du passé* (Paris, 1957), 142, note 1. [Eng. trans., *The Vision of the Past* (New York, 1966), 102, note 1.]

32. *Comment je crois,* 1934, 16; *Comment je vois,* 1948, 15. Two unpublished essays.

33. *Comment je crois,* 1934, 22.

34. *Le Phénomène humain,* 327-328. [Eng. trans., 293-294.] A much more detailed analysis of Teilhard's theology of Christ's relationship to the universe will be found in Mooney, *Mystery,* 67-87.

35. *L'Energie humaine,* 1937, in *L'Energie humaine,* 192.

36. *Esquisse d'une dialectique de l'esprit,* 1946, in *L'Activation de l'énergie,* 156.

37. *Le Dieu de l'evolution,* 1953, 5-6. An unpublished essay.

38. *Esquisse d'une dialectique de l'esprit,* 1946, in *L'Activation de l'énergie,* 155. In *Creative Union in Christ in the Thought of Teilhard de Chardin,* a doctoral dissertation at Fordham University, Donald P. Gray has analyzed with great insight the various modes by which Teilhard correlated his two faiths. Dr. Gray's book has recently been published as *The One and the Many* (New York, 1970).

39. *Note pour servir à l'évangélisation des temps nouveaux,* 1919, in *Ecrits du temps de la guerre,* 367.
40. *La Place de l'homme dans l'univers,* 1942, in *La Vision du passé,* 324. [Eng. trans., 231.]

NOTES FOR CHAPTER VIII

1. Pierre Teilhard de Chardin, *Note pour servir à l'évangelisation des temps nouveaux,* 1919, in *Ecrits du temps de la guerre* (Paris, 1965), 367. This essay does not appear in the English translation of this work.
2. This point has been well made by Joseph Donceel, "Teilhard de Chardin and the Body-Soul Relation," *Thought,* XL (1965), 373-374. Father Donceel adds that the realism of St. Thomas, though it had enormous influence in philosophy and theology, had practically none in the area of spirituality.
3. *La Vie cosmique,* 1916, in *Ecrits du temps de la guerre,* 53. [Eng. trans., *Writings in Time of War* (New York, 1967), 64.]
4. *Réflexions sur deux formes universes d'esprit,* 1950, in *L'Activation de l'énergie* (Paris, 1963), 230, note 1.
5. Letter of March 15, 1916, in Henri de Lubac, *La Pensée religieuse du Père Teilhard de Chardin* (Paris, 1962), 349. [Eng. trans., *The Religion of Teilhard de Chardin,* (New York, 1967), 243.]
6. *Le Milieu divin,* 1926-1927 (Paris, 1957), 199. [Eng. trans., *The Divine Milieu,* revised edition (New York, 1965), 152.]
7. Harvey Cox, *The Secular City* (New York, 1965), 83.
8. *Ibid.,* 265, 266.
9. *Ibid.,* 265.
10. *Lettres de voyage* (Paris, 1961), 87, 105. [Eng. trans., *Letters From a Traveller* (New York, 1962), 123, 140.]
11. *Le Christ dans la matière,* 1916, in *Hymne de l'univers* (Paris, 1961), 48-50. [Eng. trans., *Hymn of the Universe* (New York, 1965), 46-49.]
12. *Le Milieu divin,* 162. [Eng. trans. 130-131.]
13. *Ibid.,* 185. [Eng. trans., 145.]
14. *Mon univers,* 1924, in *Science et Christ* (Paris, 1965), 96. [Eng. trans., *Science and Christ* (New York, 1968), 68.]
15. *Le Milieu divin,* 123. [Eng. trans., 82.]
16. Gabriel Vahanian, *Wait Without Idols* (New York, 1964), 235.
17. *Le Milieu divin,* 166, 39, 66. [Eng. trans., 133, 23, 42.]
18. *Ibid.,* 56. [Eng. trans., 66.]

19. *La Lutte contre la multitude,* 1917, in *Ecrits du temps de la guerre,* 126. [Eng. trans., 107-108.]

20. *Pastoral Constitution on the Church in the Modern World,* art. 22, 41, 38, 40, in Walter M. Abbot, editor, *The Documents of Vatican II* (New York, 1966).

21. Letter of December 12, 1919, in *Blondel et Teilhard de Chardin, Correspondence,* ed. by Henri de Lubac (Paris, 1965), 30. [Eng. trans., *Pierre Teilhard de Chardin and Maurice Blondel, Correspondence* (New York, 1967), 33.]

22. *Le Vie cosmique,* 1916, in *Ecrits du temps de la guerre,* 7. [Eng. trans., 17.]

23. *Le Coeur de la matière,* 1950, 23, 25. An unpublished essay.

24. *Réflexions sur le bonheur,* 1943, in *Cahiers Pierre Teilhard de Chardin,* II (Paris, 1960), 61.

25. *Le Milieu divin,* 64. [Eng. trans., 71.]

26. *Ibid.,* 71. [Eng. trans., 74.]

27. For a full treatment of this large subject, see Christopher F. Mooney, *Teilhard de Chardin and the Mystery of Christ* (New York, 1966), 106-121.

28. Undated letter of 1934, quoted in *Lettres de voyage,* 180. [Eng. trans., 206.] The phrase "divine Milieu" was almost always used by Teilhard as a proper name for Christ, to indicate his physical omnipresence in the world. See on this point, Mooney, *op. cit.,* 80ff.

29. Letter of December 12, 1919, in *Blondel et Teilhard de Chardin,* 32-33. [Eng. trans., 35.]

30. *Le Milieu divin,* 92. [Eng. trans., 87.]

31. *Ibid.,* 92-93, 173. [Eng. trans., 88, 137.] Teilhard especially tries to inculcate this attitude regarding moral evil, for he was fully aware of the paralyzing effect that concentration on one's sins or the world's sins had on the people he knew. Hence he speaks of the *felix culpa* of personal sin, because "though not everything is immediately good to those who seek God, everything is capable of becoming good." Cf. *ibid.,* 88-94. [Eng. trans., 85-89.] Nevertheless, while this spiritual attitude is most important for our times, the theology of sin which Teilhard used to support it lacks that sense of serious sin as a rupture of one's personal relationship with God. Cf. Mooney, *op. cit.,* 133-142.

32. Letter of April 9, 1916, in *Genèse d'une pensée* (Paris, 1961), 124. [Eng. trans., *The Making of a Mind* (New York, 1965), 98-99.]

33. See Robert O. Johann, "Charity and Time," *Cross Currents,* IX (1959), 140-149.

34. Letter of October 23, 1923, in *Lettres de voyage,* 64. [Eng. trans., 104.]

35. Letter of September 8, 1935, in *ibid.,* 186. [Eng. trans., 207.]

36. *Réflexions sur le progrès*, 1941, in *L'Avenir de l'homme* (Paris, 1959), 96. [Eng. trans., *The Future of Man* (New York, 1964), 72.]
37. *Le Milieu divin*, 201. [Eng. trans., 154.]
38. *Ibid.*, 196-198. [Eng. trans., 152.]
39. *Le Coeur de la matière*, 1950, 2. An unpublished essay.
40. See Mooney, *op. cit.*, 52-54, 123-128.
41. *Super-humanité, super-Christ, super-charité*, 1943, in *Science et Christ*, 213, 215. [Eng. trans., 169, 170.]
42. For a fuller development, see Mooney, *op cit.*, 154-163.
43. See René d'Ouince, "L'Epreuve de l'obéissance dans la vie du Père Teilhard de Chardin," in *L'Homme devant Dieu*, III (Paris, 1964), 331-346.
44. Letter of October 10, 1950, in Henri de Lubac, *La Pensée religieuse du Père Teilhard de Chardin*, 340, note 4. [Eng. trans., 367, note 98.]
45. Letter of January 21, 1936, in *Lettres de voyage*, 197. [Eng. trans., 219.]

NOTES FOR CHAPTER IX

1. For a complete treatment of the relation between this theological speculation and Teilhard's evolutionary system, see Christopher F. Mooney, *Teilhard de Chardin and the Mystery of Christ* (New York, 1966). In its original form this chapter appeared in the Spring 1967 issue of *Social Research* and is reprinted here with permission.
2. This double criticism is made frequently. See, for example, *Le Phénomène humain* (Paris, 1955), 49-50. [Eng. trans., *The Phenomenon of Man* (New York, 1959), 53.] Hereafter cited as *PH*.
3. *Le Phénomène humain*, 1930, in *La Vision du passé* (Paris, 1957), 228-229. [Eng. trans., *The Vision of the Past* (New York, 1966), 162.]
4. *PH*, 22 [Eng. trans., 29.]
5. *Ibid.*, 49-50. [Eng. trans., 53.]
6. Letter of April 11, 1963, in Claude Cuénot, *Pierre Teilhard de Chardin* (Paris, 1958), 311. [Eng. trans., *Teilhard de Chardin*, (Baltimore, 1965), 255-256.] A similar accusation against "phenomenologists" is to be found in a letter of April 18, 1953, in *ibid.*, 426. [Eng. trans., 213.]
7. Letter of April 26, 1934, in *ibid.*, 264-265. [Eng. trans., 213.]
8. Letter of October 11, 1936, in *ibid.*, 264-265. [Eng. trans., 213.]
9. See for example: Norbert Luyten, "La Méthode du Père Teilhard

de Chardin," *Teilhard de Chardin et la pensée catholique,* ed. Claude Cuénot (Paris, 1965), 19-63; Léopold Malvez, "La Méthode du P. Teilhard de Chardin et la phénoménologie," *Nouvelle Revue Théologique,* LXXIX (1957), 579-599.

10. *PH,* 202. [Eng. trans., 183.]
11. *Le Phénomène humain,* 1930, in *La Vision du passé,* 231. [Eng. trans., 164.]
12. *PH,* 56. [Eng. trans., 59.]
13. For a fuller explanation of the role of these two energies and of the law of complexity-consciousness in Teilhard's thought, see Mooney, *op. cit.,* 38-66.
14. The word "consciousness" is never used by Teilhard as a synonym for thought, but is related to thought rather as the whole is to the part. It denotes "every kind of psychism from the most rudimentary forms of interior perception imaginable to the human phenomenon of reflective thought." See *PH,* 53, note 1. [Eng. trans., 57, note 1.]
15. *Ibid.,* 323. [Eng. trans., 289.]
16. *Ibid.,* 293-294. [Eng. trans., 264.]
17. See on this point Ernan McMullin, "Teilhard as a Philosopher," *Chicago Theological Register,* LV (1964), 15-28.
18. *Esquisse d'un univers personnel,* 1936, in *L'Energie humaine* (Paris, 1962), 70-71; *PH,* 194. [Eng. trans., 176.]
19. *PH,* 22, 25, 26. [Eng. trans., 30, 31, 32.] In this context see the interesting reference to Kant in *L'Energie humain,* 145, and the remark of Jean Hyppolite that Teilhard "was more Hegelian than I," in letter of April 24, 1957 in Cuénot, *op. cit.,* 311. [Eng. trans., 255.]
20. *PH,* 343, note 1. [Eng. trans., 308, note 2.]
21. *Ibid.,* 328. [Eng. trans., 294.]
22. *Esquisse d'un univers personnel,* 1936, in *L'Energie humaine,* 70.
23. *PH,* 199. [Eng. trans., 180-181.]
24. *Sauvons l'humanité,* 1936, in *Science et Christ* (Paris, 1965) 177. [Eng. trans., *Science and Christ* (New York, 1968), 136.]
25. *PH,* 290. [Eng. trans., 261.] See the perceptive essay of Madeleine Barthélémy-Madaule, "La Personne dans la perspective teilhardienne," *Recherches et Débats, Numéro* 40 (Paris, 1962), 66-78.
26. Jean-Marie Domenach, "Le Personalisme de Teilhard de Chardin," *Esprit,* XXXI (1963), 337-365. See Teilhard's letter to Mounier in *Science et Christ,* 291-293 [Eng. trans., 221-223], which does not, however, touch upon the questions under discussion.
27. *PH,* 247. [Eng. trans., 223.]
28. *Ibid.,* 289, 291, 292 [Eng. trans., 260, 262, 263]; *Sauvons l'humanité,* 1936, in *Science et Christ,* 178 [Eng. trans., 137]; *La Grande option,* 1939, in *L'Avenir de l'homme* (Paris, 1959), 75. [Eng. trans., *The Future of Man* (New York, 1964), 54.]

29. For a selection of texts, see Mooney, *op. cit.*, 226, note 22, and 256, note 81.
30. *La Planétisation humaine*, 1945, in *L'Avenir de l'homme*, 1959-160. [Eng. trans., 124-125.]
31. Domenach, *op. cit.*, 358-362.
32. Paul Chauchard, *Man and Cosmos* (New York, 1965), 110-112; Pitirim Sorokin, *The Ways and Power of Love* (Boston, 1954), 6, 10-11.
33. *La Messe sur le monde*, 1923, in *Hymne de l'univers* (Paris, 1961), 30. [Eng. trans., *Hymn of the Universe* (New York, 1965), 31.]
34. Roger Garaudy, *Perspectives de l'homme* (Paris, 1961), 170-203.
35. *Recherche, travail et adoration*, 1955, in *Science et Christ*, 287. [Eng. trans., 218.]
36. *Le Milieu divin* (Paris, 1957), 60-62. [Eng. trans., *The Divine Milieu*, (New York, 1960), 38, 39.]
37. Letter of January 11, 1941, *Lettres de voyage* (Paris, 1961), 268. [Eng. trans., *Letters From a Traveller* (New York, 1962), 276.]
38. Cuénot, *op. cit.*, 448. [Eng. trans., 369.]
39. *Trois choses que je vois*, 1948, 5. An unpublished essay.
40. *Ibid.*, 4.
41. Letter written in English in 1937 or 1939, cited by Claude Cuénot, "Teilhard et le Marxisme," *Europe*, March-April, 1965, 24.
42. *Le Coeur du problème*, 1949, in *L'Avenir de l'homme*, 348. [Eng. trans., 268.]
43. *L'Esprit de la terre*, 1931, in *L'Energie humaine*, 50, note 1.
44. *Le Néo-humanisme moderne et ses réactions sur le Christianisme*, 1948, 3. An unpublished essay.
45. *PH*, 300. [Eng. trans., 270.]
46. Nothing has been said explicitly in this chapter of Teilhard's relationship to modern existentialism, since his total system is an answer to the anxiety of our time. For a summary of Teilhard's own experience of this anxiety, see Mooney, *op. cit.*, 13-21.
47. Letter of June 4, 1935, in Cuénot, *op. cit.*, 180. [Eng. trans., 145.]